MOVING FORWARD

Group

Loveland, Colorado

Group resources really work!

This Group resource incorporates our R.E.A.L. approach to ministry. It reinforces a growing friendship with Jesus, encourages long-term learning, and results in life transformation, because it's:

Relational—Learner-to-learner interaction enhances learning and builds Christian friendships.

Experiential—What learners experience through discussion and action sticks with them up to 9 times longer than what they simply hear or read.

Applicable—The aim of Christian education is to equip learners to be both hearers and doers of God's Word.

Learner-based—Learners understand and retain more when the learning process takes into consideration how they learn best.

Moving Forward

Visit our website | group.com

Editor: Bob D'Ambrosio
Contributor: Marlene Wilson
Art Director: Amy Taylor

ISBN 978-0-7644-9774-2

Printed in the United States of America.

10 9 8 7 6 5 4 3 2 1   18 17 16 15 14 13

Contents

...Contents

Introduction

Being intentional about volunteer recruitment, orientation, and training sets the foundation for volunteer equipping.

When it comes to recruiting volunteers, there's a long list of ideas that simply don't work. Maybe you've tried one of these…

- You have the pastor hold the Sunday morning service hostage until someone signs up for nursery duty next week.

- You place inserts in the Sunday morning bulletins week after week after week until you get enough names to staff the Sunday school.

- You stand the cutest little girl you can find up front in the worship service asking for someone—*anyone*—to come help her understand Jesus. Extra points if her lower lip is quivering and there's a single tear creeping slowly down one cheek.

- You send letters home with all the fourth-grade boys demanding their parents take turns serving as helpers—or else. It's not until later you realize all the letters wound up as ammunition in a paper wad fight out in the parking lot.

It's no surprise that those techniques of volunteer recruitment are destined to fail. Anyone who's made a compelling announcement asking for volunteers and then stood at a lonely sign-up table suspects there *must* be a better way.

There is.

This book will examine proven approaches to place the right person in the right ministry. We'll discuss skills that will make inviting people into service easier and more effective.

Placement into a volunteer service role is one thing—helping volunteers suceed is another. We'll also examine what it means to give volunteers the type of orientation and training that's needed to be effective and accomplish great things.

When all this comes together, you have a winning formula. You win. The volunteer wins. The ministry wins. The people your ministry serves wins. Isn't that what it's all about?

Recruitment Redefined

A new way of thinking about recruitment. Trends in volunteerism. Why people do—and don't—volunteer. And what *really* motivates volunteers.

Many people think that recruiting volunteers is a matter of crafting a sales message and then putting the people who respond to work. We tuck those warm bodies into open volunteer slots and then move on.

The problem with that approach is that volunteers who enter a ministry that way don't stick. They aren't fulfilled, and they usually aren't effective. You end up right back on the same old treadmill, trying to replace people who you got to replace other people who themselves were replacements.

A certain amount of turnover will happen no matter what you do. But you can shrink turnover and increase volunteer satisfaction (yours with the volunteers, and the volunteers with their roles) by thinking of recruitment as *more* than a sales job. And by determining that just any warm body *won't* do for your volunteer ministry.

Think of recruitment this way: Recruitment is an invitation to discuss a volunteer ministry opportunity. It doesn't mean the person responding will necessarily get the position.

Notice that when you recruit with this definition in mind, the process is like a job interview, where a company selects from among a pool of talented applicants. It's not a desperate attempt to get somebody doing a job that needs to be done.

But you might be thinking: *I AM desperately seeking people to do jobs that need to be done! I can't AFFORD to be selective.*

Not only can you afford to be selective, you *must* be selective. To do anything else is to shortchange everyone in the process—the volunteers, your church, and the people who will benefit from the volunteers' involvement.

> ## You *must* be selective.

Consider what happened to a youth minister who was short a youth sponsor and was then introduced to someone who wanted the position…

"The guy looked perfect for the role," says John, the youth minister. "He was good-looking, high energy, and related well with the kids. Plus, I had so many parents telling me he'd make a wonderful youth sponsor that I felt I had to try him out."

Mistake.

After a month of service, the new 27-year-old youth sponsor decided to date one of the senior high girls.

The good news is that John happened to walk into the conversation while the sponsor was telling the girl what time he'd pick her up for their date—so the date never happened.

"I was shocked," says John. "My heart went to my throat, my stomach fell to my feet, and I thought, "am I *hearing* this? I wanted to *kill* the guy."

Nothing on the background screening had indicated the new volunteer abused children. Or sexually molested teenage girls. Or even drove too fast in a school zone. And in fact, the volunteer never *had* done any of those things.

"He just met a nice girl and wanted to take her out," remembers John. "When I told him he couldn't date the kids, he was baffled. He didn't see what the problem was. He didn't have a clue."

Would it have been worth John's time to be more selective about whom he placed in the youth sponsor role? Absolutely. And would he have been smart to sit down with the sponsor and cover the bases about what was—and wasn't—appropriate behavior? You bet.

But John was desperate for staff and wasn't sure he'd do any better if he kept looking. So he took a shortcut and bypassed the orientation and training—something he will no longer do.

"Nothing happened, but it easily could have," says John, who still serves in a position where he's responsible for equipping volunteers. "I learned a *lot* from that experience."

When you live in a world of too many jobs and too few volunteers, how can you turn down people who are willing? The harsh reality is this: Sometimes you have to go with the people you have

> "How can you turn down people who are willing?"

available. The *good* people—the people you *wish* you had—aren't the ones signing up when you pass around the sign-up sheet.

What's wrong with people these days? Why isn't anyone volunteering anymore?

Trends in Volunteerism

The fact is that people *are* volunteering—just not in the ways you may remember.

Back in the Good Old Days, when relatively few women worked outside the home, you could sign up volunteers by simply announcing a need. Back in the Good Old Days, when the work week was 40 hours long and families played badminton in the backyard after dinner, men had time to get together on Saturday afternoon to do yard work at the church building.

But those Good Old Days are gone—if they ever existed at all.

These days you're facing trends that shape how much time people are willing to volunteer and how they want their volunteer commitments structured. Your community may differ somewhat, but in general, you'll need to consider these following 12 trends when you're creating your volunteer ministry.

- **Work life is expanding—and varied.**

  How many people do you know who still work the hours of 9 to 5, Monday through Friday? Some studies indicate that only about a third of employees work those once-normal hours.

  Part-time jobs, jobs that demand travel and long hours, service jobs with irregular hours, health-care jobs that require night shifts, extra jobs, home-based jobs that blur the lines between "family time" and "work time"—these are common today. So are long commutes that consume extra hours each day.

  Many churches want to find people who'll commit for several months at exactly the time many volunteers are seeking short-term, one-shot volunteer assignments.

> People staffing your volunteer roles will be juggling jobs, families, friends, and their volunteer duties.

According to Independent Sector's *Giving and Volunteering in the United States* (Washington, D.C., Sept. 2011), 33.3 percent of persons who are employed part time volunteer, and 28.7 percent of persons who work full time volunteer. That means the majority of people staffing your volunteer roles will be juggling jobs, families, friends, and their volunteer duties.

- **Families are changing.**

  In many homes, grandparents are now raising their grandchildren. Single-parent households are far more common than they once were. The traditional definition of "family" is being stretched and redefined in many directions, and there are unique stresses with each definition. Woe to the organization that assumes there will be stay-at-home moms who will sign up to be den mothers, recess chaperones, or Sunday school teachers.

- **People seek balanced lives—and that may eliminate volunteering.**

  In an effort to live lives that include family, friends, work, and worship, many church members are intentionally opting to *not* volunteer for tasks. This isn't a lack of concern or unawareness. It's a deliberate decision to limit the number of their obligations, and for these potential volunteers, a "no" is a non-negotiable "no."

- **There's increased competition for volunteers.**

  Organizations that were once well funded by government agencies are experiencing budget reductions. Every organization is trying to do more with less. The demand for volunteer labor is increasing, which means your church members might very well have full volunteer schedules at the United Way, a homeless shelter, or Habitat before you ever contact them about serving on a church ministry team.

- **The motivation for volunteering is shifting.**

  In the 1950s and earlier, the value behind volunteering was commitment. When you signed on to teach Sunday school, you did so because you were expressing a commitment to God, the church, and the children.

  Today the values behind volunteerism seem to be compassion (I want to help and make a difference) and community (I want to be part of something bigger than myself. I want to belong and to be in a network of caring people).

  Motivation impacts *everything* in a volunteer setting, from how you invite volunteers to how you place them to how you recognize them.

- **Volunteers expect more.**

  Maybe they used to settle for that "good feeling" that came from helping others, but now they're expecting the organizations that use them to be professional, flexible, and responsive. Good enough isn't good enough anymore. Nobody expects average these days. If a volunteer experience is disorganized, frustrating, or wastes the volunteer's time, that volunteer won't be back.

- **There's a changing pool of volunteers available.**

  As Baby Boomers reach retirement age and want to do something significant, highly trained and highly skilled people are becoming volunteers. The ranks of volunteers are also growing because of layoffs and corporate downsizing. Teenagers are entering the volunteer pool because of experience with school "service learning" projects and to bolster resumés for college applications and job searches.

- **Volunteers want to shoulder responsibility, not just tasks.**

  Many volunteers bring significant leadership experience with them when they show up to volunteer. They want to be actively engaged in their roles, which means they want to use all of their skills. Electrical engineers won't be satisfied for long stuffing envelopes. Volunteers are seeking meaningful, interesting work.

  > Volunteers are seeking meaningful, interesting work.

- **There are more volunteer options available in churches.**

  As churches grow in size, the number of "niche" ministries grows. It used to be that a volunteer could work in Christian education or serve on a board. Now a volunteer can help direct traffic, handle finances, play bass in the worship band, update the church Facebook page, or serve coffee in the café.

- **Guilt is gone as a motivator.**

  "Because you should" isn't a reason people willingly accept any longer. Rather, volunteers are motivated for other reasons, and they're more willing to explicitly ask what benefits will come to them as a result of their volunteering. Volunteer managers must be able to answer the question "What's in it for me?" with clear, definite benefits that will flow to the volunteer.

- **Technology is changing volunteering.**

  It's now possible to write, edit, and produce the church's monthly newsletter without ever setting foot in the church office. Balancing the books requires an internet connection, not board meetings. And the list of technology-related volunteer roles—handling lights and sound, computer consulting, social media usage, and preparing PowerPoint presentations, among others—is growing rapidly. Some volunteer positions require specialized knowledge and thorough training.

- **The cost of training and maintaining volunteers is rising.**

  It's more expensive than ever to bring a volunteer on board at your church. The cost of a background check, the training needed to make a volunteer proficient in a role, insurance to protect the church and volunteer, and even the software for tracking volunteers is more extensive than ever before.

  It's unlikely this trend will reverse direction anytime soon, if ever.

  Please note that these trends aren't good or bad; they simply exist. They're reality. And as you plan ways to initiate a volunteer-equipping ministry or fine-tune the one that's already in place in your church, you've got to keep them in mind. Wishing there were more stay-at-home moms who want to donate a day per week to your project won't make it come true.

> "These trends aren't good or bad; they simply exist."

Why Won't People Volunteer?

Everyone who's attempted to staff a ministry with volunteers has a top-ten list of excuses they hear again and again. But the items on those lists usually boil down to two basic issues: a perceived lack of time and fear.

1. Address the perceived lack of time.

Fact: We all get 24 hours in a day, and 168 hours in a week. The amount of time available to volunteers and non-volunteers is precisely the same.

The concern about having enough time to volunteer really isn't about time. It's about the number of obligations a potential volunteer already has that make a claim on his or her time.

If a person is pulled in many different directions and rushes through a nonstop hectic schedule, it's going to feel as if there's no time to spare... and there isn't. One unforeseen incident sets off a domino effect that leaves the next ten appointments missed or delayed. There's no margin in this person's life.

> "Will this person dedicate enough time to the role to be successful?"

For each potential volunteer, there is a critical issue you must settle before you place the volunteer in a role: Will this person dedicate enough time to the role to be successful? And can the volunteer provide the *right* time? Is the volunteer available when the volunteer job needs to be done?

A busy sales professional decided to join the Big Brothers. Following the necessary interview and screening process, a first meeting was set up to introduce the volunteer to a potential match. An agency representative was present, as was the volunteer, the 8-year-old boy who was seeking a big brother, and the boy's mother.

The agency representative laid out the agency's expectations again. The big brother and little brother would meet once a week for three to four hours, meetings would be confirmed by phone 24 hours in advance, outings would be inexpensive, and all parties would stay in touch with the agency. Everything was exactly as described in earlier communications with the individual parties.

Then the mother casually mentioned that the meetings would have to be on Mondays between 3:00 and 6:00 p.m. Weekends were already booked with activities, and her work schedule was set.

The connection between the boy and the volunteer never developed. For the volunteer, Mondays were busy—especially during work hours. He could meet with the boy on weekends and evenings, but not during work hours.

The volunteer experience failed to develop, but *not* because the volunteer lacked time. It failed to develop because the time the volunteer *had available* didn't match the requirement.

As you seek to match busy people with volunteer roles, what can you do to overcome the barrier of a perceived lack of time? Here are some suggestions...

- **Segment volunteer roles so there are more, but less time-consuming, roles to fill.**

   For instance, rather than ask a Sunday school teacher to gather supplies, prepare the lesson, and teach the lesson, you might have another volunteer do the gathering of supplies. Divide volunteer roles into contained tasks, and recruit more volunteers who each do less.

- **Connect the volunteer role with another valued activity.**

   For instance, if a potential volunteer wants to spend more time with family, suggest a volunteer role that can be accomplished by a family. If the potential volunteer wants to get more exercise, suggest that the volunteer mow a yard, weed a garden, or do another exercise-oriented task.

- **Suggest that the potential volunteer sign up for a one-shot project rather than an ongoing role.**

   An airline pilot whose flight schedule won't allow her to consistently lead a small group on Wednesday night might very well be willing to give a full day some weekend when she's off. Sometimes it's not the amount of time that's a problem; it's the expectation that the same hour will be available each week.

Short-term missions are growing in popularity because they're short term—and can be accomplished by someone who's not willing to completely change his or her life. Habitat for Humanity (www.habitat.org) and Group Mission Trips (www.groupmissiontrips.com) have found ways to recruit thousands of volunteers who do remarkable amounts of ministry in short-term settings.

- **Create flexible volunteer positions that are less time sensitive.**

  It doesn't really matter if someone creates a form on your church website at 9:00 in the morning or at midnight. And if you're planning ahead, stocking up on animal crackers for VBS can happen anytime during the week before VBS begins. Be intentional about structuring volunteer opportunities so they have the maximum time flexibility possible. This won't be possible with some roles—such as leading a class that meets from 9:30 to 10:30 on Sunday mornings—but it will be possible elsewhere.

- **Create volunteer positions that don't require travel.**

  Especially for older volunteers who might be homebound or have issues with travel at night or in bad weather, look for volunteer tasks and roles that don't require travel. Some examples: making phone calls, creating follow-up packets for visitors, and creating craft packets from materials delivered to the volunteers' homes.

  When "I don't have time" emerges as an issue in dealing with volunteers, don't assume you understand what the potential volunteer means by those words. It's worth probing to see if one of the strategies listed above can manage the issue and make it possible for the potential volunteer to sign up for a role.

2. Address the fear of volunteering.

Some people shy away from volunteering because of fear. Not necessarily fear of your organization or the specific opportunities you're offering, but, rather, three other things.

Failure—If a volunteer role is poorly defined or lacks training and resources, failure is an almost certain outcome. If volunteers sense they're set up for failure, they won't feel excited about participation.

Volunteers dislike crashing and burning on projects or disappointing themselves and you. It's up to you to design the volunteer role so you can provide reassurance that no volunteer will be sent out on a limb that will then be cut off.

> If a volunteer role is poorly defined or lacks training and resources, failure is an almost certain outcome.

Abuse—*Abuse* is a strong word and may overstate the case—but not by much. When a volunteer is given an impossible task, it feels like abuse.

Jim Wideman, in his book *Children's Ministry Leadership: The You-Can-Do-It Guide* (Group Publishing, 2003), describes what sometimes happens to people who sign up to teach Sunday school. "In many churches, new Sunday school teachers are trained by getting a little lecture, handed a book, thrown in a classroom, and told to not come out until Jesus returns."

Jim describes what happens to new volunteer teachers this way: "We tell them they'll get some help, and in a couple years we *do* find them a helper. That's when we open the classroom door and are amazed when the teacher comes screaming out, quits on the spot, and disappears forever. So what do we do? We hand the book to the helper we found and throw *that* person into the room."

Small wonder someone in a church like that would be afraid to sign up to teach Sunday school. You can't quit, and there's no training. It's a volunteer's nightmare…and it's abusive.

A volunteer would only have to be mistreated that way once before deciding *never again*. And the only way to be *sure* it never again happens would be to avoid all volunteer roles.

By the way, volunteers consider it equally abusive to take them on and then give them nothing worthwhile to do.

Not being "good enough" — On a typical Sunday morning, a church member will see people preach, teach, and lead music. There may be solo instrumentalists, a band, or a choir. There may be people ushering. Perhaps there are greeters and people staffing an information desk.

And depending on the size of the church and the church's emphasis on excellence in programming, the people serving in visible roles might be demonstrating professional-level skills. They're not just singing — they're singing remarkably well. They're not just playing piano — they're playing at a level you'd expect to hear in a concert hall. They're not just ushering, they look like the concierge at the five-star hotel downtown.

The unintended message: If you're going to serve here, you've got to have the skill and polish of a pro. In our worhip band, only music majors need apply.

Is that true? Probably not...or maybe it *is* true.

A church's desire to have excellent programming creates a smoother, more enjoyable worship service. But it also discourages potential volunteers who know they can't hit the high notes or deliver a top-notch lesson. It can seem there's no place for a nonprofessional to participate.

Here are ways you can banish fear when it comes to volunteering.

- **Define roles carefully — with a full position description in writing.**

  Position descriptions provide reassurance to potential volunteers in that they know what they're getting into — and that you've thought through what you want. Solid information tends to help people see a challenge as an opportunity or adventure rather than a threat.

- **Listen carefully to concerns about the volunteer role and the volunteer's fit with the role.**

  What's behind the concern? Has the volunteer failed in another volunteer role? Has a friend failed in the role you're proposing? Is there a question of trust about how thoroughly you've described what's expected? What history is the potential volunteer carrying into the discussion? If you detect fear or suspicion, gently probe to get to the root of it.

- **Remove uncertainty.**

  Volunteers can be less than confident about participating because they know they're being "sold" on a project. Sure, you're here now—when the volunteer hasn't yet been reeled in—but will you be around when there's a problem to be solved?

  Let potential volunteers know what you'll do to help them in their volunteer efforts. Describe the support and involvement they can expect from you and other leaders. Then do what you say you'll do.

The Unspoken Barrier to Volunteering

There's another common reason people don't volunteer, though you'll never hear people actually say it: tradition.

> "Another common reason people don't volunteer: tradition."

In many churches, it's a *tradition* to simply sit in the pew. Few people ever volunteer for anything. It's a *tradition* to pay the soloists who sing on Sunday morning, the nursery workers who care for children on Wednesday night, and the caterers who've replaced the potlucks.

Inviting people to serve in ministry in a church culture that doesn't honor or encourage volunteerism is a challenge of Olympic proportions. And at heart, it's a spiritual matter.

If you're in a church where serving "just isn't done," consider doing the following.

- **Meet with the leadership.**

  Determine if your assessment is accurate. Is it true that most people won't volunteer, or is that true just of one ministry area? If the children's ministry area can't beg, borrow, or steal a volunteer but the adult ministry has a waiting list for involvement, the problem may be with the reputation or administration of the children's ministry area. Be sure you see things clearly and that you're fixing the right problem.

And if most members of your congregation *are* volunteering in service but only outside your church, that's helpful to know, as well.

- **Ask leadership to provide teaching about the biblical expectation for involvement.**

  If people truly aren't serving anywhere, ask for clear teaching about the biblical mandate to serve others.

- **Remove every barrier you can find to volunteering.**

  Some have been identified already, but consider these possibly hidden barriers, too:

  Do paid staff members discourage volunteers? It can be done by failing to design roles that can be filled by volunteers or refusing to provide information that allows volunteers to function effectively.

  Is there such competition for volunteers that it frightens volunteers away? If the new members' class is stalked by the youth pastor, children's pastor, and other staffers who are all pitching the importance of their different ministries, it may create an environment that actually repels volunteerism. To say "yes" to one staffer creates hard feelings with other staffers.

  Is there a "volunteer-toxic" environment that combines a refusal to delegate with vague or nonexistent job descriptions? It may be so difficult to come on board as a volunteer that it's truly not worth the effort.

  Are volunteers ignored? Find out when the last volunteer recognition effort was organized. If the year starts with "19–" then you've identified one problem to overcome.

- **Pray—and invite others to pray with you.**

  Is your church one that's discouraged—and, as a congregation, has no vision for the future?

  Is your church one that's defeated? Perhaps your "glory days" of attendance and impact were 20 or 50 years ago, and those who remain see themselves as defenders of a glorious tradition. Your leadership has dug in and is holding on…and that's all.

Is your church dead? There's no spark of life anywhere you look?

Pray for your church and what God wants to do with you. Ask others— whose hearts align with yours about wanting to see people involved—to join you in regular times of lifting your church up to God.

Recruitment Revealed

There's a simple technique that will revolutionize your recruitment efforts. It's powerful, simple, and you can do it without having to invest in additional books, conferences, or consultants.

And you even get immediate feedback when this technique is used.

Ready?

Here it is: *Ask people to serve.*

It's that simple. Honest.

> Ask people to serve.

One of the reasons most frequently cited by volunteers as to why they didn't get involved sooner is that nobody asked them to do so.

That *doesn't* mean they weren't aware of countless messages on serving. They may have walked past sign-up tables, sat through announcements, and flipped past the pleas for help written in the church newsletter and bulletin.

But nobody *asked* them, face to face, by name, to fill a volunteer role.

If it's increasingly difficult for you to get volunteers, consider how large a role person-to-person recruitment plays in your approach. It is far, *far* more effective than "paper-to-people" recruitment efforts.

What *Really* Motivates Volunteers

First, a disclaimer: You can't motivate a volunteer. It's simply not within your power. But you can discover what already motivates individuals and try to scratch those particular itches.

> A disclaimer: You can't motivate a volunteer.

Everyone has what Marlene Wilson calls a "motivational preference." If you can identify it, you can help each volunteer have a meaningful experience while volunteering through your program.

David McClelland and John W. Atkinson did groundbreaking research at Harvard University and the University of Michigan, respectively, which led to a theory that goes a long way toward helping you identify what motivates your volunteers. A brief listing of their seminal studies is given at the end of this chapter.[1]

Fortunately, Harvard professor George Litwin and his research assistant, Robert Stringer, Jr., helped translate the McClelland-Atkinson theory and applied it to organizations in their book, *Motivation and Organizational Climate*. Marlene Wilson adapted these ideas to working with volunteers in her book, *The Effective Management of Volunteer Programs,* and the following synopsis appears courtesy of Harvard Division of Research, Graduate School of Business and Volunteer Management Associates.

McClelland and Atkinson were curious about why one person's favorite job was another person's least favorite and why some people liked to figure things out on their own while others wanted clear directions.

Starting with the premise that "people spend their time thinking about what motivates them," they conducted extensive studies checking out what people thought while walking, eating, working, studying, and even sleeping. They discovered people *do* think about what motivates them, and they identified three distinct motivational types: Achievers, Affiliators, and Power (or Influence) People.

Let's take a closer look at those three motivational types.

- **Achievers value accomplishments and results.**

  They like to set goals and solve problems. They want to know where they're headed and want things to happen in a timely way. They *hate* having their time wasted.

Achievers tend to be well-organized, prefer deadlines, are moderate risk takers, and are often articulate. They like "to-do" lists. They depend on their pocket calendars and electronic organizers. And if achievers have a leader who's poor at delegation, they'll go crazy.

If an achiever responds to a project they think is significant and they discover it's just a small task, the achiever's motivation immediately deflates. In fact, unless they're extremely committed to the cause, you'll lose them.

In churches resistant to change, where achievers have no room to grow and stretch, you'll find them coming in one door and going out another. You can utilize and attract achievers by learning how to use ministry teams effectively. Search for achievers with good delegation skills, and they'll form excellent teams around themselves.

- **Affiliators are "people people."**

  They're sensitive, nurturing, and caring. Interacting with others and being part of a community is what motivates them. They care less about the work being done than about the people they're doing it with. They're easily hurt, so leaders need to know that affiliators will require more of their time. However, it's time well spent because affiliators make church a good place to be. They're the ones walking up to visitors and striking up conversations.

  Affiliators are good barometers about how things are going in your ministry. They know how people are feeling about things. They're also good persuaders, listeners, and public speakers. They make excellent interviewers, members of listen-care teams, or leaders of small groups.

  And they're great choices for projects like mass mailings. Get a group of affiliators together with a pot of coffee, and they'll have the mailing done before you know it—and enjoy the process because they chatted the entire time.

- **Power People come in two varieties: McClelland categorized them as *personal* and *social*.**

Both types like to think about having impact on people and outcomes. They think long-term and are good strategists. If you want to enact change, find some power-motivated people and get them on your side. If you convince them, they'll spend their time thinking about who they need to influence and how they need to do it.

Personal Power People use their power on *people* usually through manipulation and intimidation. They think in terms of win-lose, and if they perceive someone else is "winning," they instantly assume they're losing. They're comfortable with conflict—and tend to create a lot of it!

> In the church, personal power people can be toxic.

In the church, these people can be toxic. If someone has left your church bleeding, there was probably a personal power person involved. These are also the people who can quickly crush programs and new ideas.

Social Power People like to influence and impact others in a win-win way. Convince a social power person of your vision, and they'll move mountains to see your project happen. The reason they can do this is because they see power as infinite and self-renewable. The more power they give away, the more they get. Therefore, they aren't threatened by the success of others. Their goal is *your* success. How the church needs these people!

By the way, social power people are the best at dealing with personal power people because they aren't intimidated by them. *Never* send an affiliator to deal with a personal power person.

Please understand that most people have some characteristics from each of these motivational types, and an individual's primary motivational style may change over time and within differing situations. Marlene Wilson reports that she has exhibited all three styles.

When she was a homemaker while her children were young, she was an affiliator. When she became a program director, she shifted into achievement. She used to enjoy thinking about program goals or how to write a book or produce a video series. Now she sees herself as a social power person. She finds herself thinking, *"How do I influence things that matter? How do I use whatever time and energy I have left to have the most impact on the things I care most about?"*

You can motivate people with these three styles by placing them in appropriate settings. For instance, an affiliator may make a wonderful receptionist, so long as the job doesn't also require a great deal of pressure to get e-mail and data input done on a tight schedule.

And you can use insights drawn from these types to create appropriate recognition for individual volunteers, too.

1. Seminal studies contributing to this paradigm include: David C. McClelland, *The Achieving Society* (Princeton, NJ: D. Van Nostrand Company, 1961); John W. Atkinson, *An Introduction to Motivation* (Princeton, NJ: D. Van Nostrand Company, 1964); John W. Atkinson and N. T. Feather, *A Theory of Achievement Motivation* (New York: John Wiley and Sons, 1966).

Promoting Volunteer Involvement

How to effectively craft a message and attract people to your volunteer ministry. Ten critical questions. The most effective invitation process ever.

Marketing your message of serving in ministry simply means this: deliberately telling your target audience the benefits of serving in your church and community.

The term "marketing" sometimes has a negative association because it's the same word used to describe how tobacco companies create smokers, whiskey companies create drinkers, and car manufacturers put their super-sized models in garages.

> 'Marketing' sometimes has a negative association.

It would seem that in the church, where it's understood that everyone has an ability, interest, or passion to share for the common good, where everyone is called to be active in ministry, and where discipleship is an expectation, there would be no need for "marketing" service opportunities.

After all, shouldn't church people be *looking* for service opportunities?

Well…yes. But people often *aren't* looking. And if they are, there's a lot of competition for the slice of time they have available for volunteering.

If you want to be heard and have people respond, it's important that you target an audience you want to address. Be intentional about crafting a message that cuts through daily clutter and makes an impression.

The best way to be sure that you are effectively communicating with people you want to address is to create a marketing plan. With a marketing plan, you won't waste time and resources talking to yourself, to the wrong people, or to nobody at all. You'll make the critical decisions up front that will direct how, when, and where you communicate about the volunteer opportunities in your church. You won't find yourself answering the questions a marketing plan addresses when it's a crunch time and you're stressed.

> "You already have the information and resources you need to create a marketing plan."

Here's the good news: You already have the information and resources you need to create a marketing plan. You won't need to go hide out for a month digging through church records or hire an expensive expert to pull together a serviceable plan. You can do it.

And we'll walk you through the steps.

How to Create a Marketing Plan

First, let's clear up a couple of misunderstandings about marketing.

Marketing is *not* selling.

Marketing is simply a deliberate process of getting your message out to the people you want to hear it in a clear, concise manner.

Marketing is *not* manipulation.

The goal of your communication should never be to somehow trick people into serving. That's completely counterproductive. You end up with people you don't want as volunteers, and your volunteer ministry gains a reputation that will keep good people away.

Marketing is *not* just for people with MBAs.

There's nothing terribly complicated about what you'll be doing, but it will require your making decisions. Since you can't do everything ("Let's take out a full page ad in the newspaper announcing we need nursery workers!"), you've got to decide what you *will* do—and your marketing plan is where you narrow down your communication options.

Recruiting is *not* a once-per-year event. If your church limits marketing and recruiting to a few weeks per year, perhaps as you head into the fall, you're limiting your effectiveness. You need volunteers all year, and people enter your congregation all year. So why wait to put those new people to work?

Plus, if every volunteer position comes up for renewal at the same time, you're almost guaranteeing a training nightmare as you have a large percentage of staff exit and other people come on board.

Finally, remember the wise words shared by an unknown marketing genius: *out of sight, out of mind*. If the message of serving falls off of the congregation's radar screen the majority of the year, it will be treated like a temporary distraction—not an integral part of the congregational life.

To create a marketing plan, you must answer ten critical questions. Let's look at these carefully.

1. What is the purpose of your volunteer-equipping ministry?

You will want to create a purpose statement, but before you tackle that, be sure you've got a mission statement in place. It's best if you create one in the context of a core team, and you'll find step-by-step help in the book *Jump Start* (Group Publishing, Inc., 2013) about how to craft a mission statement.

But here's a quick explanation: A mission statement communicates who you are, what you do, what you stand for, and why you do what you do. It's clearly articulated, widely understood, and truly supported by your church leadership, your volunteers, and by you. Your mission statement is the banner you hold up to rally the troops and to let potential volunteers know what you're about.

Before you market your "product" (presumably connecting people with volunteer opportunities and helping people be successful in those opportunities), you've got to be able to describe what you're doing. The clearer you are, the better you'll communicate with your target audience.

> "The clearer you are, the better you'll communicate."

Your mission statement is an integral part of your marketing plan. If you *don't* have a mission statement—or the mission statement you have is vague or not compelling—take time to revisit it or to create a statement when you've assembled your task force.

Your volunteer ministry's *purpose* is tucked away in your mission statement. It's the problem you want to solve or the thing you want to accomplish. It's the reason you exist as an organization or a ministry.

Some questions that might help you get at your purpose in order to craft a purpose statement are:

- Who does your volunteer-equipping ministry serve?
- What services does your volunteer-equipping ministry provide to those you serve?
- What is unique about your ministry?

Be sure your purpose clearly identifies why your ministry exists and that it's inspirational to your paid staff, volunteers, and the people you're serving. A test: Run the purpose statement past your most dedicated volunteers—the ones you wish you could clone. How do they respond to it? Does it capture what motivates them to be involved?

And be sure your purpose statement can keep everyone focused on what's truly important in your ministry.

2. What can you say—in a "sound bite"—about serving in ministry?

You probably won't be interviewed by a national news network this week, but if you were and you had to sum up what you do in just a few seconds, could you do it?

A "sound bite" is a short statement that captures the spirit of what you're doing to connect volunteers to ministry. It's a quick, catchy phrase that a news story would run on the air. And it's the sort of phrase that will stick with people who hear about serving in ministry.

Words to Avoid When Inviting People Into Ministry

When crafting your marketing message, there are words you'll want to avoid. Good news: Here's a short list you can delete from your vocabulary before they get you in trouble! (Bad news: You'll probably discover other things to avoid as you work with volunteers.)

Worker. Who wants to be a "worker" in a ministry? The term denotes one of those bees who hauls pollen around all day so the Queen Bee can live in luxury. Call people team members, or staffers or by their first names—but *don't* call them "workers."

Should. If this is your answer when people ask you why they might volunteer, you're dead in the water. Nothing turns off most people more than being told they *should* do something. That's a "push" word. Dig a little deeper and cast a "pull" vision that draws people *toward* the decision to volunteer.

Obviously. Okay, it's clear to you that people need to volunteer. But don't assume it's clear to them. They've not volunteered in the bell choir for 40 years and haven't run out of oxygen yet, thank you very much.

Duty. Ouch. This is a cousin to *should*. The clear implication is that failing to do what you've been asked to do is not just saying "no." It's *shirking* your duty.

Desperate. That you're desperate for a volunteer raises some questions you'd rather not raise: Why are you desperate? What do other people know that has convinced them to refuse? What aren't you telling me?

Anyone can do it. Do you mean it's so easy that it's meaningless or that someone with the skills of a houseplant could accomplish the task? Either way, it's insulting.

(continued on next page)

When creating a sound bite for your marketing, make sure it's brief, catchy, and packed with exciting, descriptive words. Make it memorable, and have it tell the essence of what your ministry does.

These sample sound bites will give you a taste of what you're after:

"Lend an ear, gain a friend."

"Help grow kids who care."

"Make a friend for life."

"Serve a child, serve the Savior."

> A 'sound bite' is the sort of phrase that will stick with people....Go borrow an elevator and give your sound bites a try.

There will be many times that you have a brief opportunity to market your volunteer ministry. Be able to do so in ten seconds or less.

Some professional salespeople actually prepare what they call "elevator presentations," brief pitches that can be delivered in an elevator as it travels from the tenth floor to the ground floor. There's no room to show visuals, so it's the power and focus of the words that have to connect. Go borrow an elevator and give your sound bites a try. You'll be ready when the pastor points to you and says, "Let's let our equipping ministry leader take 20 seconds to tell you about it."

3. Who is your target audience?

There was a time when most volunteer invitational messages were aimed squarely at stay-at-home moms. As noted earlier, that's a shrinking percentage of the population. These days you'd better think again about whom you want to reach with your marketing message.

This isn't a small thing. You must communicate your message in words that the audience understands and highlight benefits the audience cares about. The language you select must connect with that audience.

Please note that you may have several campaigns running at the same time. You may be targeting the following audiences.

Internal audiences—such as your pastor, board, or other governing body. Your message might be that there's a need for their support, endorsement, and involvement. You might also be building enthusiasm among the paid church staff for working with volunteers. You might be soliciting leadership's help in fundraising.

External audiences—as you recruit for additional volunteers or a specific type of volunteer. You may be asking for time from people or goods and materials from businesses. You might be asking young drivers to sign organ donor cards or elderly people to donate used eyeglasses. You might want a volunteer to take over the junior high youth group or someone to help coordinate weddings scheduled at your church building.

Who's your audience? What do you know about those people? What do they care about? What's their situation in life—are they likelier to be married or single? Parents or not parents? Working, retired, or between jobs? Young or old? Do they have transportation, or are they homebound? Are they leaders or followers? Are they conservative or liberal? Do they value stability and tradition or innovation and change?

And are there times they're so involved with other things that they simply won't pay attention to your message? For instance, if you're recruiting Sunday school teachers *on* Christmas morning, your timing is way, way off.

> "You want to speak their language."

The more you can identify the people you want to reach, the easier it is to reach them. You want to speak their language.

And don't think that this sort of market segmentation communication is something new. Consider what the Apostle Paul said about sharing the gospel:

> *Though I am free and belong to no man, I make myself a slave to everyone, to win as many as possible. To the Jews I became like a Jew, to win the Jews. To those under the law I became like one under the law (though I myself am not under the law), so as to win those under the law. To those not having the law I became like one not having the law (though I am not free from God's law but am under Christ's law), so as to win those not having the law. To the weak I became weak, to win the weak. I have become all things to all men so that by all possible means I might save some. I do all this for the sake of the gospel, that I may share in its blessings.* (1 Corinthians 9:19-23)

Of course, you may be designing a marketing campaign that you want to reach everyone in your church. They're all over the map when it comes to age, health, and employment status. How can you target a message when there's no specific group of people to whom you want to aim your message?

Think again. There *are* commonalities in your church.

For starters, they all go to your church. They've accepted some common truths and beliefs. They probably all live in relatively close proximity. Many of them may know each other. They may agree on fundamental doctrinal issues. If you want to recruit five people to paint the Christian education classrooms, they've all seen the peeling paint. If you want to recruit ten people to do a community outreach program, they all know the neighborhood. If you want to recruit twenty people to feed and house members of a visiting choir, they all know their way back to church when it's time to deliver the choir members for a performance.

The nature of what you're trying to accomplish will help you find the common traits in potential volunteers, and help you select which volunteers to target.

Which leads to the next question…

4. What are your assumptions about your audience?

You aren't communicating in a vacuum. People in your audience already have feelings and beliefs about serving. They already have feelings and beliefs about themselves as volunteers, about you as a volunteer recruiter, about how volunteerism fits in your church, and about serving itself.

> "People in your audience already have feelings and beliefs about serving."

Depending on how people feel and think, you may need to tailor your marketing message. For instance, if you're the sixth person this year who's tried to break through apathy and get someone—*anyone*—to volunteer, it's probably not a good idea to start with a pulpit announcement. Why? Because that's what all five of the other people did—and everyone in the audience has already said "no" five times.

You need to start somewhere else.

What can you discover or surmise about your audience? What do they know about the volunteer ministry? Is it positive or otherwise? Where did they get the information they have? How would they describe what a typical volunteer experience is like in your church?

Describe how you believe people feel and think about volunteering in your church. One description might be as follows:

> *Volunteering is for the old people in our church because they have lots of discretionary time. Once you sign up for a volunteer role, you're stuck in it until you die or Jesus comes back. Volunteers get honored once a year at a banquet, but that's about it—you never see them being thanked other than that. I should volunteer—I feel bad that I don't—but I'm a volunteer in other places like the Scouts and the kids' school. Except I don't think the pastor would count that as real volunteering because it's not at church.*

If those are thoughts running through your audience's mind, shouldn't your marketing message take these thoughts into consideration and address them?

It's not just the thoughts and feelings of the audience that impact your message; your thoughts, feelings, and assumptions play a part, too. Some of your assumptions might include...

- People are willing to give their time and resources if they're invested in a specific church program such as Sunday school, youth group, home visitation, or outreach.

- People expect to get something of value from their volunteer experience.

- People volunteer because they're asked directly.

- Volunteers are important people who have tremendous value.

- The church staff assumes that most volunteers aren't well trained or very reliable.

- The church staff thinks volunteers are nice to have but aren't to be included in decision making.

- Some church staff thinks volunteers are more trouble than they're worth.

- Volunteers tend to quit unless their egos are stroked continuously.

What do you assume about volunteers? How do those assumptions aid or hinder your marketing message?

Four Tips for Creating an Effective Invitation to Ministry

1. Communicate a vision.

It's one thing to ask someone to "be a worker" in vacation Bible school; it's another to ask if someone would like to have the privilege of having an eternal impact for Christ in a child's life.

Communicating your need for volunteers won't motivate people; that's *your* problem. But inviting someone to join you in doing something important that will have an impact—*that's* worth doing.

2. Test your message.

What you easily understand may not be easily understood by others. Avoid slang, insider information, and abbreviations (for instance, not everyone knows that "VBS" stands for vacation Bible school)—unless you use them strategically to connect with your target audience.

3. Communicate benefits without dwelling on them.

People want to feel noble when volunteering, not as if they're signing up just to get something in return.

4. Make it easy to respond.

How can someone get more information? Make it simple to follow up with a contact point. Provide a phone number, website, brochure, physical information kiosk—several options that provide the same simple, clear information. Make it easy to take the next step, and the more personal you can make the contact point, the better.

That said, sometimes there's value in making it *difficult* to respond.

(continued on next page)

Four Tips for Creating an Effective Invitation to Ministry *(continued)*

At a local church, two sign-ups were underway after each worship service. One table was for the parish blood drive, and the recruiter was as close to the main door as possible so he could speak to everyone passing by. He had a sign-up sheet and schedule with him.

The woman recruiting teachers for an upcoming catechism class set her table up across the parking lot, inside the parish school, down the hallway in a classroom.

The blood donor recruiter told the woman, "You know, if you move your table over here by mine, you'll get a lot more people to sign up."

The woman smiled sweetly and said, "I'm not after people who need it to be convenient to sign up. I want people who are motivated enough to find me. You're after large numbers, so you're recruiting with a net. I'm after a very special sort of volunteer, so I'm fishing with a line."

What approach best suits your recruitment effort: a net or a line?

A rule of thumb: Spend more time on vision than logistics—it's the vision that will convince a potential volunteer that the role is both doable and worth doing.

5. What goals do you have for your marketing?

You need to define the outcomes of your marketing efforts if you hope to achieve them. And the more specific you are, the better you'll be able to determine if your plan got you where you wanted to go.

When you've finished your marketing efforts, what do you want people to know about your volunteer ministry? to say about it? What will your target audience be doing differently than what they're doing now? How many new volunteers will you have recruited or will you have reenlist? What evidence will point to the fact that your message was heard?

Keep in mind that if your marketing plan calls for you to bring people on board gradually, your plan should reflect that outcome in an appropriate timeline. It does you no good to recruit 100 people today if you have nowhere for them to serve. If you expect to have 100 positions gradually open up throughout the coming year, write your marketing plan in such a way that it calls for you to recruit people at gradual intervals so nobody's time is wasted.

Be definite about your goals and write them clearly. If you don't aim at something specific, you won't know if you've accomplished what you set out to do—and that makes evaluating your efforts all but impossible.

> **Be definite about your goals and write them clearly.**

When setting marketing goals—or any goals—include the following elements.

- **Make goals specific.**

  "I want people in our church to know there are lots of ways they can volunteer" is too vague to be of any practical use. Force yourself to become more specific by determining *which* people you want to have knowledge…*what* they'll do to demonstrate they have knowledge… *where* they'll go as a result of having knowledge (to a volunteer orientation, hopefully!)…*when* they'll take action based on their knowledge…and *why* they'll care about the knowledge they've gained.

  Anything you can do to sharpen and focus a general marketing goal helps you accomplish it—because you know what you're aiming at.

  A more specific way to phrase the goal presented above might be: "25 members of our church will attend a volunteer orientation program on February 10, and 21 will be placed in volunteer roles by February 25."

- **Create goals that are possible to attain.**

  "Everyone in our church will be serving in a volunteer role this year" is a great goal. It's a *wonderful* goal. But is it likely you'll attain it?

  Probably not.

  There's nothing wrong with aiming high, but if you aim *too* high, you'll just get discouraged. It's not necessarily a failure of your faith to set a goal that's more attainable. Should it be a challenge? Yes. Should it require faith? Certainly. But should it be realistic and attainable? Absolutely.

  Goals must be achievements you're willing and able to work toward. If you set the bar high, that's motivational. If you set the bar so high there's no hope of your reaching it, that's unfair to you and anyone who's willing to help you.

  > "Only you can determine if a goal is too high, too low, or just right."

  If you have 45 people serving in volunteer roles this year, perhaps it would be a more realistic—yet challenging—goal to write, "As of April 10, 75 members of our church will be actively involved in volunteer roles."

  Only you can determine if a goal is too high, too low, or just right. Do you believe that with God's help and hard work you just might reach it? Then it's probably a good goal.

- **Create goals that have measurable outcomes.**

  One measurement is time—set deadlines for the various steps in your marketing plan. If you intend to make an announcement from the pulpit on Sunday, which Sunday will it be? If you'll be personally contacting everyone in the church directory, when will you get to all the A's? All the B's? When will you finally be calling Zack Zuckerelli?

  How many volunteers do you want to enlist? By when?

  Marketing goals need observable results. You can count noses when it's time for a volunteer training event—so count noses. You can count the number of phone calls or personal visits you make, so count them.

One reason you make marketing goals measurable is to be able to track progress toward meeting them. Be sure to include time deadlines with each goal and subgoal. The accountability is necessary.

> "Marketing goals need observable results."

Also, put a *name* next to each observable goal and subgoal. Who is responsible for making it happen? If it's everybody, you're in trouble. Only when someone specific is accountable for achieving a goal will it actually happen.

As you move forward over time, it's likely you'll have to adjust your timing, tweak your budget, and reconsider which parts of your marketing plan require revision. Having observable goals lets you know where you are in the process.

A note: If you adjust your plan, keep track of those changes and update your written marketing plan. It's your master-planning document. Take time to document why and when you made adjustments—that information will help you do a better job of planning in future marketing cycles.

6. What are the benefits your volunteers can expect to receive?

Let's start by differentiating between features and benefits.

A feature is a *characteristic* of a product or service that's inherent in that service or product. For example, in a new car there are many features— power steering, air conditioning, and a gas gauge are among them.

A benefit is the *advantage* the user of the car receives because of the features. Power steering allows the driver to maneuver the car more easily. Air conditioning allows the driver to be comfortable in hot weather. And the gas gauge lets the driver avoid running out of gas and having to hike to the closest gas station!

What are the benefits your volunteers can anticipate receiving that you can include in your marketing message?

There was a time that few people would admit to volunteering for any reason other than pure altruism or discipleship. It was all about helping those less fortunate and serving God.

Now the "What's in it for me?" question is raised more directly. It's not that people are no longer altruistic, but they're quicker to acknowledge that they have other motivations for volunteering, as well. They're comfortable with the notion that it's okay to profit in some way from volunteer service.

This kind of profitability seldom comes in the form of money, though some volunteer service qualifies for tax breaks. Rather, volunteers also want to receive a nontangible benefit from their hours of service.

Not every volunteer role provides the same benefits. Not all benefits are equally desirable to each volunteer. But if you can present a variety of possible benefits for volunteers to consider, it may sweeten the deal when it comes to recruitment.

Among other benefits, these are some that may be available to volunteers:

Increased skills—If a teenager is planning to babysit for extra money, it never hurts to say that she's a regular volunteer in a church nursery.

Increased contacts—When someone volunteers, he or she makes contacts that can be leveraged for business or social opportunities. And in addition to those pragmatic concerns, friendships can quickly develop in a volunteer setting. Volunteering is a way for those new to a church to be more quickly integrated into the faith community.

Increased knowledge—Someone who wishes to grow in a skill set may gain valuable experience in graphic design, sound engineering, or another area of expertise.

Increasing career potential—Networking that happens in a church volunteer setting can lead to new employment or a reference that will enhance a resume.

Increasing self-awareness—By interacting with people in a volunteer setting, volunteers can expand their personal horizons and explore new situations and challenges. Volunteers often learn much about themselves.

Feeling accomplishment—Playing guitar in the worship band or serving in the church drama ministry might well satisfy a desire to perform that can't be met apart from joining the local community theater.

Satisfying a desire to give something back to the community or church—It's possible that someone who's volunteering at a homeless shelter today may have been a resident there just a few months ago. It's not uncommon for someone who's a tutor today to have benefited from a tutor's help in the past. There's a tremendous sense of satisfaction in helping another person.

Changed focus—If a volunteer is ill, depressed, lonely, or adjusting to loss in life, helping others can provide relief.

Raised self-esteem—Volunteers may feel better about themselves and their abilities because they're helping others. Also, they'll feel they are making a valuable contribution and may feel needed.

Recognition—A plaque, pin, or something to hang on the wall of the study or wear on a lapel may be the extrinsic reward that a volunteer craves.

What are the benefits that will be available to volunteers participating in your volunteer ministry? How have you made that information available?

Note that some volunteers consider it crass for you to recruit on the strength of what's in it for the volunteers themselves. They want to think of themselves as primarily altruistic even as they consider which benefits might flow back to them. It's a wise volunteer manager who delivers the benefits that volunteers desire but treats those volunteers as if they're acting on the most noble motives possible.

7. How do you intend to deliver your marketing message to the target audience?

There are nearly endless possibilities for ways to deliver your message.

You might attend scheduled church meetings and speak to people in groups such as worship services, committee meetings, and classes. Or you might send literature to people at home. You could call everyone directly. Then there's the face-to-face meeting, which is normally far more effective than any other technique at sharing your enthusiasm about the volunteer ministry—and recruiting additional volunteers.

Some factors that might influence which communication channels you select include...

The task for which you're recruiting volunteers—If your goal is to recruit enough people to move chairs out of the church sanctuary after the morning worship service this weekend, you won't need to provide much training—or seek a long-term commitment. In that case, an announcement and call for a show of hands will probably do the job, especially if the call for volunteers comes at the end of the worship service in question.

> ...the more complicated the task or rare the volunteer skill set, the more direct your communication will need to be.

Do you need an eye surgeon willing to go on a medical mission trip or twenty people willing to bake two dozen cookies for the next potluck? Generally speaking, the more complicated the task or rare the volunteer skill set, the more direct your communication will need to be.

The number of volunteers you need—If you're in a church of five thousand people and you need three volunteers for a fairly simple role, stopping into one adult class to recruit volunteers may accomplish the goal.

If you're seeking hundreds of volunteers, you'll need to contact lots of people. An e-mail blast is one option, but so is training a team of volunteer recruiters who will make personal contacts on your behalf.

Your budget—Your marketing plan will cost more than just time, though staff time and volunteer hours may be the most expensive item on your budget. Every activity will have a financial cost associated with it.

If you expect to do mailings, contact the post office or a mail center to determine the most cost-efficient way to make use of letters, brochures, or newsletters. If you intend to create teams to do marketing activities, then also figure in food and other reasonable costs.

Make the budget information available to people who are responsible for marketing activities, by the way. They need to know how much money—and time—they have to spend.

> ## Your marketing plan will cost more than just time.

The time available—When you're planning the Christmas cantata and it's July, that's one thing. When the river's hit flood stage and the Red Cross needs people to haul sandbags, that's another situation altogether.

There are times a "phone tree" can be effective because the need for volunteers is immediate, and the cause so compelling very little explanation is needed.

Seek to plan far enough ahead when recruiting and using volunteers that you do *not* need to make use of instantaneous recruitment strategies. They may work once, but there's a diminishing return. Remember what happened to the proverbial boy who called "wolf" once too often: He lost the ear of his audience and suffered for it.

And when it comes to getting the most "bang for your buck," there's one way to reach your target audience that has far more impact than any other: *word of mouth*.

There's no more powerful way to market your volunteer ministry than through current volunteers. When a current volunteer tells friends that it's a great thing to serve, that's an invitation message that no number of slick brochures can equal.

Your current volunteers are your absolute best recruiters. They know the positions, they know your culture, and they know people like themselves.

Be intentional about word-of-mouth advertising. It may not occur to your current volunteers that they can recruit additional volunteers unless you encourage them to do so.

Here's how to create a successful word-of-mouth marketing campaign. It costs you nothing…but brings huge returns!

- **Create a super volunteer environment.**

  Unless current volunteers love spending time in their roles, they'll never recommend a friend to do the same. Ask yourself: "Is what we do worthy of praise? Is how we do it worthy of praise? Are the results we're seeing worthy of praise?" If the answer to any of those questions is less than an enthusiastic "yes," you're not ready for a word-of-mouth marketing campaign.

  Why? Because what is being said won't be positive.

  When your process is praiseworthy (ask your volunteers to let you know when that happens), then it's time to go to the next step.

- **Find and thank champions.**

  Not every volunteer will be willing to talk up serving in ministry. Identify those who will—and those who are effective at bringing in new referrals and volunteers. Go out of your way to thank them and encourage them to keep up the effort!

- **Bring your champions into the information loop.**

  You don't want them giving misinformation—or old information. Be sure you brief them and provide every possible reason that they could recruit a new volunteer for you.

8. What marketing content do you want to deliver?

You have a purpose statement. You've written your sound bites. You've identified what matters to your target audience. You know which benefits you can offer to your volunteers. You have an idea how you might want to connect with your target audience.

But all that makes very little difference if you have nothing to say.

Firm up the content you'll deliver in your marketing message. What is the central message you want to deliver?

When marketing your volunteer ministry, there are some things you simply *can't* promise.

- Volunteering won't necessarily make participants rich—at least monetarily.

- Volunteering won't necessarily make participants younger—at least on the outside.

- Volunteering won't necessarily make participants more attractive to the opposite sex—but it certainly couldn't hurt!

The fact is that most of the benefit-promising marketing messages used to sell investments, skin cream, and baldness remedies just aren't available to you...but it's no real loss.

You *can* with integrity communicate that in volunteering, there's deep fulfillment and meaning. That through volunteering, a person can impact lives forever—and for the good. That through the touch of volunteers, people who have no homes

> "...in volunteering, there's deep fulfillment and meaning."

can find housing, people who seldom smile can find joy, and people who were once unable to read now can be employable.

You can craft a message that talks about significance, not sensuality. That's a message Coca-Cola® would love to own—but they don't. They never will. It's *your* message to share because the work you do connects people with people at a profound level.

Don't focus on what you can't say and promise. Focus on what *only* you can say.

As you craft your message, remain mindful of these points...

- **Keep your message simple.**

  No one wants to have to decipher your message. Be sure your audience never has to work hard to sort out what you're saying. And make responding to your message very, very easy.

  For instance, rather than making volunteers figure out that to sign up they can call the church office and leave a message at 555-CARE, just list the phone number. Especially among older volunteers whose bifocal vision no longer appreciates small print, being forced to peck out the right buttons on a phone isn't appreciated.

> Keeping your message simple sounds easy, but in fact it's very difficult.

Keeping your message simple sounds easy, but in fact it's very difficult to resist the temptation to complicate things. The benefit of simplicity is that it focuses on the quality and truth of your presentation, not on the gee-whiz theatrics of PowerPoint text swinging in from every possible direction on the screen.

Simplicity eliminates distractions and lets your audience focus on the central message.

- **Make sure your message reflects the tone of your volunteer ministry.**

  If it's fun to volunteer, say so. Show happy people interacting with other happy people in brochures and video clips. Talk about the friendships that have developed.

> If it's fun to volunteer, say so.

At one church in a northern state, the youth group got together after each heavy snowfall and shoveled the walks and driveways of elderly church members. The goal was to get to a home and shovel it— always at night, when the youth group members could meet—without being detected by the resident.

"Operation Snow" was a successful volunteer service project, but few in the youth group would have described it as such. To them it was the chance for buddies to pile into a station wagon and have fun while sneaking around at night. Friendships were the big draw; helping others by shoveling was a secondary outcome.

When recruiting for new volunteers, Operation Snow crew members talked about the sneaking—not the shoveling.

- **Be accurate in crafting your message.**

  While it's true that some volunteer positions save lives and make the world a better place, some volunteer positions fall a bit short of that. Folding bulletin covers is not quite as heroic as teaching the toddlers. Both roles are important; but don't portray the bulletin-folding job as on a par with taking the gospel to China. Never exaggerate, because people aren't fooled, and you'll only diminish your credibility.

  Rather, describe the benefits of folding bulletin covers when you do it weekly with three friends around a table at the church building; it's a social time that includes fun, friendship, and donuts.

- **Grab the attention of your target audience.**

  That's easier said than done, but you need to make sure you are creating marketing messages that cut through the clutter of information overload and impact audiences.

  Make the message personally relevant. If you're an 81-year-old widow, it's unlikely any marketing effort on behalf of the young marrieds Bible study group will motivate you to attend a meeting.

  People tend to pay attention to things that have implications in their own lives, especially if what's being marketed appeals to their own personal goals, values, or felt needs.

  One need felt by almost everyone everywhere is the need for more time. If you can honestly portray your volunteer ministry as making a huge impact in a limited amount of time, that's going to be well received. Don't ask people to "set aside a full week to support missions in Haiti by going to serve people."

  Instead, ask them to "impact lives in a short-term, one-week mission trip."

  See the difference? The first message sounds like a huge investment. A *full week*? Who's got a *full week* to spare? The second message sounds like less of a time commitment, though both messages refer to the same seven days.

We also tend to pay attention when people portrayed in marketing efforts look like us, act like us, and seem to care about the things we care about.

Here's how you can put that tendency to use: On your volunteer Web page and in your announcements, use people who resemble the folks you're trying to reach. If you want to build attendance in your family night activities, show families. If you want leaders for the men's group rafting trip, show men who look like they could handle a raft.

Make the message enjoyable. People are drawn to things that make them feel good. That's one reason guilt is a poor motivational tool—it simply doesn't feel good. People avoid it.

You can make your marketing message enjoyable in several ways:

Excellent visuals—Don't settle for dark or muddy pictures or static visuals. Take the time to capture images that are attractive, fun, and of top-notch quality. It's worth the investment. And don't forget the power of showing your volunteers in action.

Engaging sound—If someone is doing a voice-over for a prerecorded announcement or recruitment video, use a voice that's easy to understand and sounds attractive. That's not to say you have to hire an expensive voice-over artist; using too "slick" a voice might actually backfire and alienate your audience. You don't need a voice professional—just someone who can speak with enthusiasm and clarity.

If you use music in your marketing, be sure the music you select is appropriate to your message and your audience. Music hooks emotions; be sensitive to what emotions you might be snagging. And respect copyrights when you select music—if it's illegal to use a song and you do so anyway, you signal to your audience that you aren't to be trusted. After all, you've just broken the law.

> "Never make your audience work hard to decode what you're saying."

Easy readability—If you do a print piece, make it easy to read. Don't let a designer overpower your message with creative design. In the same way, use simple words in a straightforward fashion. Never make your audience work hard to decode what you're saying.

And a word about humor: Avoid it—It's dangerous, and a joke or cartoon in your brochure grows tiresome after a few readings. Can humor be used effectively and make a marketing message enjoyable? Absolutely. But realize that what's funny to one person isn't funny to the next person. Why take the risk?

Make the message unpredictable. It's predictable to *you*, of course, but it shouldn't be easily predicted by the person on the receiving end of the message.

If a message is novel, odd, or unexpected, it grabs attention because it's involving and new. Those two qualities require a great deal of creativity, of course, but the impact is worth the effort—*so long as the novelty doesn't obscure the message.*

Use this approach sparingly, and always test it before incorporating it widely in your marketing. It has great potential to confuse as well as amuse.

- **Use testimonials.**

  In every e-mail, video, PowerPoint presentation, and announcement about volunteer opportunities, include a testimonial. Why? Because people are skeptical when *you* tell them about a volunteer position. As the person recruiting volunteers, *you* need volunteers, right? So it stands to reason you'll say anything to recruit someone and solve your problem.

  That means you have low credibility simply because it's perceived that you will benefit when someone raises a hand and volunteers.

  But when someone *else* says that volunteering is rewarding—someone perceived to be objective—then the words carry more weight.

  Is this fair? No. Is it necessarily accurate? Of course not—but it's real. Why do you think companies selling weight loss programs always show you a happy customer who recommends the program?

Take this a step further. When it's time to announce serving opportunities, be sure it's a *volunteer* who makes the announcement.

> ## Collect testimonials from your dedicated volunteers, and keep them on file.

Collect testimonials from your dedicated volunteers, and keep them on file. Start now. You can use them when the opportunity presents itself, but not if you haven't got them in hand.

And here's a bonus: When a volunteer gives you permission to use his or her testimonial, it builds greater loyalty in the volunteer providing the glowing words.

Here are five tips for using testimonials effectively in your marketing:

- The time to ask for testimonials is toward the *beginning* of a volunteer's experience. There's a "honeymoon period" in most volunteers' involvement. That's the time when volunteers are likely to be most positive and when the volunteer is most in touch with the benefits the experience is bringing to his or her life.

- The more specific the testimonial, the better. It's one thing to say "Serving in the nursery is good" and another to say "Serving in the nursery lets me help families build a spiritual foundation in the precious children the families entrust to me."

- Ask volunteers to mention your purpose or mission in their testimonial. If your ministry to special-needs children is designed to build relationships as well as provide education, ask the volunteer to say so—if it's true in the volunteer's experience.

- If the person giving the testimonial is credentialed in a relevant way, include the credentials. It's great that a parent likes your Sunday school. It's especially great if a parent who's *also* a professional educator likes your Sunday school.

- Always, always, *always* get permission to use testimonials; never assume.

9. How will you evaluate your marketing efforts?

Your marketing efforts will grow stronger if you incorporate the classic feedback loop used by businesses when they track marketing impact: Action, Observation, Adjustment, Next Action.

Here's how it works...

Action describes the effort you make to market your volunteer ministry. For example, you launch a campaign to staff the choir with capable singers.

Observation describes your checking back to see if you were successful in meeting your marketing objectives. Are there enough sopranos or tenors?

Adjustment describes the tweaking you'll do in light of the results of your marketing efforts. If you were able to recruit all the women singers you needed but you didn't land any men, you might want to redefine your target audience or at least adjust the channels of communication you're using.

Next Action describes the new approach you're using. After giving it time to have an effect, you'll again observe the outcome...make adjustments... and act again.

Note that some evaluation is built right into the system because you identified desired marketing objectives that are observable and easily checked. (Good for you! Here's where the hard work is paying off!)

> "Some evaluation is built right into the system."

However, some other information will require digging.

Your budget, for instance—how are you doing? Are you under, on, or over? And how are you doing when measured against your timeline?

10. What trends and realities threaten your success?

When motion pictures transitioned from silent films to "talkies," even some top actors and actresses found their careers were suddenly over. Why? Because now that their voices could be heard, they lost their appeal.

Clara Bow, who had enjoyed a hugely successful career in silent films, fared less well on the silver screen when her thick Brooklyn accent was audible. Within a few short years, her film career was over. Technology had killed it.

Technology impacts your volunteer ministry, too—but how? Is it helping you or hindering you? How can you harness it to use it to your advantage? Consider not just the trends discussed at the beginning of this book, but the following list of threats and opportunities.

- **What trends in your community are working for or against volunteerism?**

  If your local high schools require volunteer service for students in a civics class, how can you position your church so it is a recipient of volunteer hours? You wouldn't use part-time unchurched teenagers in your midweek program, but you can leverage the class requirement with your own teenagers to let them fulfill the requirement as they explore church ministries.

  And perhaps the new swing set you want built in the play area could be constructed by unchurched kids?

  The economy also has an impact as adults find they're either more—or less—available to volunteer hours for projects.

- **What organizations are competing with you for volunteer hours?**

  Perhaps it seems uncharitable to think of other worthwhile organizations as competition, but you're all looking for volunteer involvement, and there's a limited pool of volunteer hours.

  What organizations are your primary competitors? When you talk to people who tell you they're already involved in service, where are they volunteering? You may discover that the local hospital auxiliary or library board is staffed with people you'd love to have leading small groups in your church.

  The questions you need answered are these: Why is volunteering for your competition so attractive? What are the benefits received by those volunteers? What can you learn from other organizations about how to structure your volunteer ministry?

- **Are changes happening in your community or church?**

  Things change—and your marketing message may need to change with them to match a shifting demographic or environment.

  Has your church had a large influx of older people? younger people? homeschoolers? people who are wealthier or less wealthy than your existing membership? Is your leadership shifting direction regarding

  > "Things change— and your marketing message may need to change with them."

  worship style, number of services, or approach to Christian education? Change isn't a bad thing, but it can certainly impact your volunteer ministry.

  The pastor of a church in the West came up with a great solution to fix the problem of an overcrowded sanctuary: Go to two services. The parking lot congestion would be lessened, the congregation wouldn't be sardined into the pews—it seemed like a "no-brainer" when he suggested it to the church board. The pastor wanted to make the change in 30 days.

  Fortunately, several board members happened to be people who have volunteer recruitment functions in the church. Both the children's church and Sunday school superintendents pressed the pastor for details: What would happen to their programs?

  The pastor thought for a moment and then shrugged. "You'll do two Sunday schools and two children's church programs, I guess."

  The church did make the change—not in 30 days, but eventually—and the superintendents did double their volunteer staffs to accommodate the change. But had the change been made in just a few weeks, as the pastor proposed, it would have been chaos.

  Stay on top of changes that will impact your volunteer ministry. For community information, talk with local business reporters and local chambers of commerce. Real estate agents often see trends develop early on, as well.

  To stay in touch with changes in your church, become an active participant on decision-making boards. Volunteer to serve there, and you'll be amazed how quickly you get in the information loop!

A Brief Summary

Creating a marketing plan is the best way to be assured that your marketing efforts will be coordinated, focused, and consistent. And to create that plan you need to answer these ten questions:

1. *What's the purpose of your volunteer ministry?*
2. *What can you say—in a "sound bite"—about your volunteer ministry?*
3. *Who is your target audience?*
4. *What are your assumptions about your audience?*
5. *What goals do you have for your marketing?*
6. *What are the benefits your volunteers can anticipate receiving?*
7. *How do you intend to deliver your marketing message to the target audience?*
8. *What marketing content do you want to deliver?*
9. *How will you evaluate your marketing efforts?*
10. *What trends and realities threaten your success?*

Don't rush the process of answering these questions. Any time you invest in creating a marketing plan will be returned many times over as you avoid off-target campaigns, last-minute decisions, and wasted efforts.

Keep your written marketing plan where you can refer to it often. It's your blueprint for marketing success. You'll want it handy.

Though there's no particular format a marketing plan should follow, we've provided some worksheets on pages 184–189. Use them to help you walk through the process described above.

Communicating about your volunteer ministry clearly and regularly is a key to successfully involving people in ministry opportunities. But *which* ministry opportunities? There may be no shortage of people in your church willing to help out with the Easter Festival, but when the Missions Fair rolls around, there's a distinct echo in the room when you ask for volunteers. Nobody responds. You're talking to yourself.

And why is it that your volunteers in one area of ministry seem to stick forever, effectively serving others and glorifying God, when you can't keep a Sunday school teacher for more than six months?

The answers to those questions can become complex, but there's an obvious place to start: Are people in the right positions? If they aren't, you can count on frequent turnover, burned

> **Are people in the right positions?**

out volunteers, and a distinct lack of enthusiasm for volunteerism in your church. When a square peg is pounded into a round hole, it's no fun for either the peg *or* the hole.

The solution: Place the right people in the right roles.

And you can accomplish that with interviews.

Interviewing Prospective Volunteers

How to get yourself and your church ready. Building a team of interviewers. The four-step interview process explained.

The context in which most of us have encountered interviews is when we've tried to land a job. And with few exceptions, the interviews have been nerve-wracking experiences.

We spend the days leading into the interview composing answers to the questions we most expect to hear from the personnel manager who's sitting behind a desk, pencil in hand as she fires off one question after another.

My biggest weakness? *That's probably my tendency toward being a work-a-holic* (a trait we secretly hope will be viewed as a virtue by a potential employer) *and maybe my near-obsession for excellence.*

The reason I left my last position? *It was a mutual decision, based on the changing demands of the marketplace.* (I'd have had to learn to actually use social media, but I won't mention *that.*)

Interviews tend to be carefully choreographed experiences, with the person being interviewed determined to reveal only what's most positive and likely to impress the interviewer; it's a sales presentation, with the sole goal of getting a job offer.

Meanwhile, the person doing the interviewing is attempting to kick over rocks and see what's hidden beneath. Does the interviewee have the skills needed to be successful? Will he fit into the corporate culture? Is there something lurking just beneath the surface that would be helpful to know—but is being concealed?

> ❝ Interviews tend to be carefully choreographed experiences. ❞

What's missing in many interviews is a desire to understand and be understood—to lay cards on the table and see if there's a good combination.

No wonder when many churches hear that interviews are essential for a well-run volunteer ministry, eyebrows shoot up. After all, if people want to volunteer, why not just let them? They already know what they want to do, right?

Not necessarily.

Let's take a look at what volunteer interviews are—and what they aren't.

The Volunteer Interview

Volunteer interviews aren't an experience in which the involved parties are trying to avoid being honest and open. Just the opposite—they're helpful *only* if everyone at the table is seeking the same goal: *to put the right person in the right role.*

> "Potential volunteers... usually don't know the complete range of volunteer roles available to them."

Here's the rub: Potential volunteers—people who've decided to commit time and energy to serving in and through your church—often don't know what's really involved in each volunteer role. And they usually don't know the complete range of volunteer roles available to them.

Consider: On a typical Sunday morning a typical church member—let's call him Bob—may see only a few roles being filled by volunteers. The greeters, ushers, and people who take up the offering are probably all volunteers, as is Bob's Sunday school teacher. And it's probable the people in the worship band are volunteers, too, but that's about it. If Bob doesn't see himself in any of those specific roles, he may decide there's nowhere he fits as a volunteer.

What Bob *doesn't* see is the administrative assistant in the church office on Monday morning. The altar care coordinator who organizes a team that keeps the front of the worship center visually interesting. He never sees all the boards meet to do the business of the church, and the follow-up and visitation teams aren't on Bob's radar. The people who write and prepare the bulletins and newsletters aren't obvious, nor are the six guys who keep the building and grounds in tip-top shape.

The youth sponsors are serving elsewhere in the building, as are most of the children's ministry leaders. And someone's going to count the money in the offering plates and handle church finances on Sunday afternoon— though Bob won't see that happen.

Bob isn't even aware that the church has periodic short-term mission trips or that the big room downstairs with all the groceries in it is a food pantry for the community.

Had Bob turned around to look, he'd have seen Susan running the sound board and John recording the pastor's sermon for distribution to shut-ins, who will be visited on Monday evening. Dale and Patty deliver those tapes and a healthy dose of encouragement every week.

There are search and personnel committees, small group ministries, singles ministries, and college ministries Bob knows nothing about—and they're all run by volunteers. A prayer team is praying for the morning worship experience even as Bob sits in church, but he doesn't know it.

The wedding Bob will attend next Saturday at the church will be coordinated by a volunteer, but Bob won't be aware of the hours Nancy has put into making sure everything is just right for the bride—and the bride's mother.

Bob has placed himself on the sidelines as a volunteer, not because he's apathetic but because he has no vision for the scope of your church's volunteer ministries.

You think Bob's a slacker. After all, he's an elementary teacher who refuses to teach Sunday school, although he's a natural. After asking him twice to take over the second-grade class and being turned down flat, you're wondering about Bob's commitment. How can a Christian be so callous about serving God?

Here's what you don't know about Bob: He's tired of teaching. After 23 years in the classroom, the last thing he wants to do is spend weekends doing the same thing he does all week long.

But he *is* an avid photographer. He often wonders why the church doesn't do more with the projection unit that's hanging from the ceiling, but he's never thought to ask. And he's just gotten a grant from the State to develop a training program for the teachers in the district. Bob's a Master Teacher who actually enjoys helping teachers fresh out of college master the real-world skills they need to deal with challenging kids.

You don't know Bob—and he doesn't know the volunteer opportunities in his own church. Not the ones that would excite him and give him the chance to pursue his passions.

So Bob sits. Week after week. And your corporate worship experience isn't blessed with visually dynamic photographs to accompany the singing. Your struggling Sunday school teachers don't receive a seminar that would build their skills and increase their effectiveness.

How many Bobs are there in your church?

Would you like to get them involved?

The interview process is one way to do it. At an interview Bob would be able to express what he's passionate about—photography, training, and whatever else God has wired him to get jazzed about—and to hear the range of places he could put that passion to use. He'd get connected.

That's what volunteer interviews do—connect people with volunteer roles. They help put the right people in the right ministry role—to the benefit of the volunteers, for the good of the church, and to glorify God. Volunteer interviews *aren't* about judging people in an effort to eliminate them from service opportunities.

> "Volunteer interviews help put the right people in the right ministry role."

Volunteer interviews are also a wonderful place to do ministry. At church we spend much of our time listening. We hear sermons, teaching, and music. Plenty of information gets beamed our way. But how often do we get to be *heard*?

In the setting of a one-on-one interview with potential volunteers, you have the privilege of entering into the lives of brothers and sisters in Christ. You get to ask questions that get at what matters most to people and then hearing what they have to say. The potential volunteers get valued and *heard*—and that's ministry. Consider it "inner-viewing."

How to Get Started With Volunteer Interviews

Before you dive into doing interviews, there are some things you need to do. Building an effective volunteer ministry is a process, and you'll sabotage your efforts if you do things out of order.

For the interview process to be effective, you need to be ready in two ways...

1. You need to be ready personally.

A question to consider: Do you *really* believe that everyone has something to offer in ministry? Truly, down deep, cross-your-heart-and-hope-to-die believe that God has gifted everyone with a skill, passion, talent, or ability that can be used to bless others and glorify God?

Because if you have any doubts about that, it's going to show in your ability to interview potential volunteers.

Ask God to impress on your heart *his* heart for letting very imperfect people do ministry in his name. It's one of the ways God shows us grace: He lets us do significant things that have eternal consequences.

Not one of the people you interview as potential volunteers will be perfect. Their skills won't be perfect. Their experience won't be perfect. Their thinking and demeanor won't be perfect. And that's as it should be—because *we aren't perfect people.*

> **You're going to have to see people as God sees them.**

So adjust your expectations and proceed accordingly. You're going to have to see people as God sees them, and place them accordingly. You (and/or your team of volunteer interviewers) must understand the goal of the process: *to get the right people into the right ministry.*

It's that simple.

You won't be attempting to sell anyone on a particular job that desperately needs to be filled. God already knows that position is open, and he has someone in mind for it—but not necessarily the person you're interviewing. It's far, far better to leave a volunteer job empty than to fill it with the wrong person.

You won't be offering career counseling or spiritually admonishing people to "name and claim" abilities, skills, or passions they don't currently have. God may choose to develop new attributes in people, but that's between them and God.

You *will* be carefully, prayerfully attempting to discover the uniqueness in each person you interview. You'll be presenting a variety of volunteer positions that might be of interest to the person you're interviewing. You'll seek to be clear, nonjudgmental, and reassuring.

Your goal is to get the right people into the right positions. Are you ready to put that goal first in your interactions with potential volunteers?

2. Your church needs to be ready.

If 50 people raised their hands today and volunteered to show up next Sunday morning to help, where would you use them? Are you ready to give them the information they need to be effective? What would you do with a flood of volunteers?

A flood is exactly what might happen if you proactively interview people in your church and unleash the volunteer potential that's simmering out there in the pews.

We've long sighed and lamented how the old "80/20 rule" seems to be the eleventh commandment in the church. We congratulate the 20 percent of the people who do 80 percent of the work, then wonder what could ignite a fire under the other 80 percent of the people who just show up and sit there.

Well, there's no sense getting people recruited if you're not ready to follow up. That will frustrate everyone.

There are eight ways you'll want your church to be ready before you begin interviewing volunteers.

- **Your church leaders must be ready to share responsibility and power.**

    Not every church truly wants volunteers in significant positions. Sometimes it's fine if "new people" set up chairs and tables for the church social hour, but to make a suggestion about how to revitalize that event, you have to have been born into the church. The advice of "newbies" isn't welcome.

    If you've asked leaders of ministry areas to tell you what volunteer positions they want filled and each position you've received is an entry level slot, that tells you something: Apparently there's not a willingness to share power. Or there's a deeply held belief that volunteers can do tasks but not lead people.

    Those are not good signs that your church will be a culture where volunteers can grow in their skills and abilities. Before you continue with implementing volunteer interviews, meet with church leadership and explore any issues that might be fueling their concern about giving volunteers power and authority.

- **You have ministry descriptions in hand.**

    Until you have completed position descriptions—preferably written by the leaders who will supervise the volunteer roles described—you're not ready to interview volunteers. Why? Because you aren't ready to put the right people in the right roles. You don't truly know what's involved in the positions. You can't answer volunteers' questions.

And you aren't absolutely sure you have the buy-in from the leaders in every ministry area. A hesitation to fill out ministry descriptions can be one indicator of a lack of enthusiasm for the volunteer placement process.

Ministry descriptions are vitally important. A sample position description is on page 190. Use it as an example to teach your leaders how to create position descriptions for existing and proposed volunteer positions.

- **You have a team of volunteer interviewers.**

  Depending on how many interviews you need to conduct, a team approach to the task is essential. For the role of volunteer interviewer, it may actually be best *not* to ask for volunteers to fill the role. It's such a specific role that you may do better to handpick people to do the task.

  When Marlene Wilson wanted to build a team of volunteer interviewers in her church, she sat down with her pastor, and they looked through a church directory.

  "We checked the 10 to 12 people we individually felt would be the best candidates," says Marlene. After determining who had the skills to be effective, the candidates were personally contacted individually and asked to consider taking on the role. Each candidate agreed.

  The result speaks to the power of a personal invitation to serve.

  Here are the qualities Marlene Wilson suggests you look for in appropriate candidates...

  Someone who is a genuinely friendly and approachable person—The ideal candidate is likely someone who has a broad network of friendships and acquaintanceships already. They're engaging and warm.

  Someone who cares about people—Your top candidates may be serving in people-helping roles already, or working in the social sciences. The value of caring about people can be expressed in many ways, but it should be in evidence.

  Someone who is a good listener—Test this for yourself. Engage a potential candidate in conversation, and pay attention to how the individual communicates empathy, warmth, and respect. Does it *feel* as if the person is listening? Do you hear follow-up questions that signal comprehension? Does it *look* like the person is listening? Is the candidate focused and attentive? leaning forward and making eye contact?

Listening skills can be taught (and should be!), but you may not have time to do so before the interviews begin. Look for candidates who have a high degree of competence in this area already.

Someone who is trustworthy and with whom people will feel comfortable sharing personal information—This is really a two-fold requirement. The person must, in fact, be able to be trusted with information. Someone who is a gossip won't make a good volunteer interviewer. And the person must be *perceived* as trustworthy by others. Otherwise interviews won't reveal much because interviewees won't be open. See page 190 for a sample position description for this role.

- **You've decided whom to interview.**

  Churches approach this issue in a variety of ways. Some churches begin with a church-wide interview process, connecting with every member. That's the ideal, but depending on the size of your congregation, it may be impractical.

  Other churches interview people who pass through the new members class and build a base of information that way. Still other churches begin the process with current leaders and those who aspire to leadership positions.

  Mindful that your goal is to identify the abilities, skills, and passions that are available to do ministry in your church and that you want everyone to have the opportunity to be effectively involved in ministry, the more people you interview, the better.

  Start small, if necessary, but look forward to including as many people as possible. And don't forget that you are interviewing *all* the membership—*including* youth and young adults. Young people have been given God-given abilities, skills, and passions, too. Don't forget to help them find significant, meaningful ministry opportunities.

- **You're ready to collect and safeguard information.**

   As you do interviews, you'll be collecting personal information. Generally speaking, you need to treat it as confidential personnel information.

   Before you begin interviewing, know where hard copies of the interview sheets can be kept in a secure environment. Know who will have access to the information—electronically or in hard copy. It may seem like a minor detail, but where *will* you put hundreds (or thousands) of pieces of information so they're secure and still available to the right people?

   Decide now what information storage and retrieval system you will use, *before* you collect information. If you're the person functioning as the Director of Equipping Ministries—at least in part of your church's programming—let this be your responsibility. You'll reap the benefits if you see that it's done well.

   If possible, use computer software or Web-based data management systems to record and retrieve information. It requires keying in data, but once you've captured it, you've got it forever. Updating addresses and phone numbers is simple, as is sorting information.

   You may already have a software program designed to track pledges, contributions, attendance, and other administrative functions. See if that program can be adapted. If not, conduct a quick Web search for programs—there are dozens of them, always being updated.

   Remember to set up different security levels so more than one user can utilize the software and only appropriate people can get at sensitive data.

> "Buy only what you'll use...and then use it."

Sound too expensive? If you buy a software program and don't use it, it's very expensive. *Buy only what you'll use... and then use it.* Nothing is more expensive that a needless technology purchase.

   If you want an inexpensive, down-and-dirty approach and you don't intend to ask for sensitive information, ask a computer-savvy volunteer to set up a simple database in Microsoft Access or another database software. Even Excel spreadsheets are sufficient for small churches.

Some questions for you to consider before purchasing software:

- Is it Web-based or installed to specific computers?
- Does the proposed software meet your present needs, exceed your needs, or greatly exceed your needs?
- Can the software meet your needs if the size of your church doubles?
- Is it easy to use?
- Who'll use the software? What do those people think of the choice?
- Is training provided? By whom? When? How often?
- What kind of on-going support does the vendor provide? At what cost?
- Can multiple users access the software at varying security levels? How? Can information be accessed from home?
- Is your current computer hardware adequate to use the software? What upgrades might be required? Are you willing to make them? At what cost?
- Does purchasing this software contribute to your ability to fulfill your mission and meet your goals? In what ways?

- **You're ready to respond when unexpected information is revealed.**

  It may not happen often, but it will happen: You or one of your team of volunteer interviewers will discover uncomfortable information about a church member.

  Generally, you aren't required to divulge what you discover to a local law enforcement agency unless you discover the individual is being hurt, is hurting or plans to hurt someone else, or is doing something illegal. Those are broad guidelines, though.

  Determine what your approach will be before you begin interviewing people. What is your church policy? The policy

> "Determine what your approach will be before you begin interviewing."

recommended by your insurance carrier? What does the law require in your area?

Do the homework now, mindful that interviews conducted with potential volunteers are an official function of your church's program.

Not every piece of unexpected information will necessarily trigger a call to law enforcement or social service authorities. But sometimes it *should* trigger a referral to a capable, qualified care-provider like a pastor or counselor.

It was during an interview with a potential children's worker that one interviewer, Kim, asked the question, "What is it about this church that attracted you?"

The woman being interviewed became quiet and stared at her hands as a long moment passed. "At least here the pastor hasn't made a pass at me yet," she said finally, in a still, small voice. Then, eyes on fire, she leaned toward Kim and hissed, "That's what happened in my last church. I hope he rots in hell."

"It was like she turned into a different person," Kim remembers. "She took a couple of long breaths, shook her head, then with a smile, looked back up at me said, 'Well, then, any more questions?'"

Oh, yeah. Kim had a *lot* more questions—but none she was qualified to ask and process with the potential volunteer.

They finished the interview. Then Kim suggested that before the woman enter into ministry at the new church she consider addressing the issues that she had with her experience at the last church.

"I told her that we'd walk through the process with her every step of the way, and I looked forward to offering her a choice of volunteer positions. But she couldn't serve joyfully out of an abundant life when she wasn't experiencing one."

The woman heeded Kim's counsel and accepted a referral to the church's counseling ministry. A year later she was on board as a volunteer.

"She's doing great," Kim says, "But she wouldn't have been if we hadn't interviewed her and given her some direction. She'd just have *appeared* to be doing great."

What would you do in a similar situation? How would you refer her? Decide now so you are ready.

- **Your church is ready to provide background screenings for potential volunteers.**

  The days when screening volunteers was the ultimate "extra mile" effort of ultra-careful churches are over. It's now something that needs to be part of your standard procedure. It protects your church, the volunteers who serve through your church, and most importantly, it protects children and youth.

  Three decisions you need to make:

  What level of screening do you need? In this world of computers you can arrange to have someone screened for practically anything. And not every volunteer position needs the same sort of background screening.

  For instance, if Jerri is going to be handling the church checkbook, you'll want to know that her credit history and her use of money have been screened. Has she proven to be a capable steward in the past?

  If Dave wants to work with a small group of children on Wednesday night, his use of credit is probably less important than whether he's been convicted of a crime, and if so, which crime.

  You can arrange for background screenings in each of the following areas, and more:

  Identification—Is the person operating under an alias?

  Criminal records—Has the person been convicted of a crime?

  Credit checks—Is the volunteer on a solid financial footing? This can be a general indicator of responsibility and financial skills.

  Education and employment verification—Has the person lied about credentials or previous employment?

  Department of Motor Vehicles—Is the person to be trusted transporting children or teenagers on trips?

  Sex Offender Registry—Is this person required to report to the state sex offender registry? Why?

You want to strike a balance that makes background searches affordable and effective. Screen by position rather than person. Decide which position requires checking and the information that should be checked.

Contact your insurance provider, and ask for guidelines. That will let you know what level of screening is generally recommended and may also qualify you for a rate discount because you've put the procedure in place. Contact other churches in your area, too. What sort of screening do they require? Why did they settle on that level?

What happens if you find that someone has been convicted of a crime? What crimes will disqualify someone from volunteering in a specific area, and which crimes aren't a problem? After all, getting three speeding tickets in a year is one thing if Larry wants to volunteer in the bulletin stuffing ministry, and quite another if he wants to drive the church bus.

And get in touch with several screening providers. If you're a member of Group's Shepherd's Watch, you can get screenings at a variety of levels at a significant discount. Take advantage of this opportunity—the savings on screenings alone can more than pay for your one-time membership fee.

Who will you screen? Not every volunteer role involves the same risks. Generally speaking, if a volunteer has contact with children or youth, that volunteer needs to be screened. Discuss other guidelines with your insurance carrier, other churches, and the screening provider you hire. Again, if you're a member of Group's Shepherd's Watch, ask for guidelines from that organization, too.

You'll need to decide what to do if a potential volunteer is new to your area. Will you screen both locally and in that person's previous place of residence? What if, after several years of service, a volunteer switches from a role where there's been no contact with children to the role of fourth-grade Sunday school teacher?

It's critical that you put policy decisions in place before you begin interviewing volunteers and that once those policies are in place, you *never make an exception.* Perhaps Mrs. Wazniak *has* been teaching children's church for 35 years. That's wonderful—give her a certificate of appreciation...and a screening.

How will you advertise that you screen volunteers—and when?

Screening is a safety net—your last chance to keep someone who has already lied to you twice (you asked about convictions on your application and in the interview, right?) from having access to the people you serve and to your other volunteers.

People who have been convicted of a crime tend to fear screenings. They know if they're listed in a sexual offender database that their names will pop up. They know if they've been imprisoned or involved in the court system that it's going to come out. So if they know you're going to screen them, they tend to not even attempt to volunteer.

So announce that you'll be screening at the interview stage of your recruitment and placement process. Why? So people have a chance to tell you about their issues, rather than hiding them from you.

If a potential volunteer says, "Look—I can tell you right now that if you screen my records you'll find out I spent a year in jail for car theft when I was 19 years old. That was 23 years ago, and I've long ago repented. I've not taken so much as a stick of gum that wasn't mine since, and I never will. God has changed my life."

That's a very different situation than someone who chooses to remain silent, waiting to see if your screening turns up a past conviction.

Let potential volunteers know early on that screening is mandatory if you intend to screen them. You'll need their approval, and if someone refuses, you may have kept a wolf out of the sheep pen.

> "Let potential volunteers know early on that screening is mandatory."

What's your plan for screening potential volunteers? Is it in place? And have you and your team already gone through the process?

It may be that to do what you're doing you don't need to be screened. It would save your church money if you weren't screened. You've never been arrested or convicted of a crime and you know for a fact you'll come up clean when you're screened.

Do it anyway, and here's why: You'll be able to tell anyone who is offended by being asked to go through a background check that you've been through the same procedure. That fact will stop a lot of arguments before they start.

Yet, you may find that if you *start* screening volunteers, you offend the faithful volunteers who have served for years. How can you navigate that situation?

Explain that everyone will be screened—and include *everyone*. Even the pastor!

Explain that results are confidential, and detail how information will be safeguarded.

Be clear on what levels of screening you're including for various volunteer positions. This will reduce fear among people who have had ancient run-ins with the law, or who fear embarrassment about past decisions.

Talk about the church's need to be viewed as a safe place by visitors who don't know the character of long-term volunteers. It's not a personal thing; it's a sign-of-the-times thing.

Stand firm. Seek to understand a volunteer's concerns, but if the decision is that everyone will be screened, everyone will be screened.

Determine how you'll go about responding if someone is found to have a criminal background. Will you separate volunteers from service? Will you keep volunteers in place if they've demonstrated healing and repentance? Will you offer volunteers who are screened out of one position the chance to serve elsewhere?

- **You're ready to make a handoff to the appropriate volunteer leader.**

  Once a potential volunteer is interviewed, where will you send the person? In each area of ministry where a volunteer will be used, there must be someone designated to do the follow-up interview. As you'll see in the next section, *you* won't actually offer anyone a volunteer position. You'll simply refer a volunteer to an area where you think they'll flourish. It's up to someone in that area to determine if the volunteer and a volunteer role are a fit.

If in your best judgment you think someone would make a great youth volunteer, is the youth ministry director ready to follow up? If not, don't send anyone to the youth department until that leader *is* ready.

Being "ready" comes down to this: Are resources in place for training and orientation that will make the volunteer successful? Have you removed as many institutional and personal obstacles to volunteering as possible? Do you have a compelling vision for what God will do through and in you as volunteers grow involved in new ways?

Is your marketing message tight and focused? your strategy for marketing set? your planning finished?

Yes? Then contact the people whom you think will make good interviewers, get them on board, and begin training them.

How to Train Your Interview Team

First, a principle to embrace: *The more your interviewers do at the front end of your interview and placement process, the less you will have to fix later.*

It's true. Interviewers are key players in the process. They have an enormous influence on whether potential volunteers eventually become practicing volunteers. You want your team of interviewers to be as effective as possible.

And to be effective, your team must have both information and skills. The data you can pass along in printed form, and it's probably best to do so in a three-ring binder. Why? Because you'll be updating it frequently. Whether you have a team of one or one hundred, decide how you'll go about getting updates into the hands of your team, and formalize that process.

Here's what your team must know...

- **Interviewers must know about your church.**

  Give your interviewers a copy of your church's mission statement and vision statement. Provide copies of your volunteer ministry's mission and purpose statements, too. Discuss them thoroughly, including the interviewers will be cooperating in helping bring those missions and purposes to life.

  Be sure your interviewers know about the major ministry areas and initiatives in your church and how those ministries wish to be described. Your interviewers are gateways for volunteers entering church ministries; if their information is spotty or incomplete, it will show in the quality of referrals made.

  If at all practical, have the leaders in those ministry areas meet your interviewers. As a potential volunteer is interviewed and then referred for a follow-up interview and placement, you want the process to be as seamless as possible. It all works best when there's at least some relationship between the people in the process.

  Consider creating a notebook of information for your volunteers, and make sure information is consistent across every volunteer's notebook. While different interviewers will have different styles, the experience should be equally informative.

- **Interviewers must know relevant policies and procedures.**

  Where do surveys go when they're completed? What tools are available for introducing potential volunteers to possible position matches? What's the timeline from the completion of the first interview to the next step? What *is* the next step? How do you make a referral? Those are the sorts of practical questions your interviewers will have—and they'll need answers.

  You'll enhance interviewers' comfort level if you anticipate at least some of the questions they'll have and proactively provide information. Then ask what other questions they have and provide that, too. One church leader has this philosophy: "Any time I hear the same question twice, I create a policy and print it out."

You may not want to go to the trouble of creating a handbook, but the information should certainly go into an updated "Frequent Questions" sheet in your interviewers' notebooks.

Interviewers must have skills, and among these are three skills that are essential for a successful interview. Here's what your team must be able to do…

- **Interviewers must be able to put people at ease.**

  Part of this skill is to conduct interviews in a setting that's free of interruptions and is physically comfortable. It may be a room or office at your church, but it can just as easily be a coffee shop where you can sit in a quiet corner booth. The chief requirement is that you find a place you can talk for 30 or 40 minutes without the flow of the conversation being broken and without being overheard.

  If you *do* use an office, avoid having a desk separate the interviewer and potential volunteer. Set the phone so it won't ring. Communicate in every way throughout the duration of the interview that nothing is more important than the person being interviewed.

  But even if the lighting is fine, the temperature perfect, and the chairs comfy, people being interviewed may still feel ill at ease.

  What *really* relaxes people is how interviewers conduct themselves. Is the interviewer rushed or relaxed? Is the interviewer open and respectful? Is the interviewer able to converse easily and listen carefully? Does the person being interviewed feel important and heard or perceive that the interviewer is just plodding through paperwork?

  > "What *really* relaxes people is how interviewers conduct themselves."

  Remember, the interview is an opportunity for the interviewer to minister to the potential volunteer. Your interviewers must be primarily people-focused, not task-oriented, as they conduct interviews. As they master the interview process, they may, in fact, choose to not even take notes unless it's absolutely necessary.

Notetaking breaks eye contact and may make the potential volunteer uneasy. It's best if interviewers can remember what was said well enough to fill in the paperwork immediately after the interview ends.

Also, coach interviewers to speak clearly and explain things patiently, preferably without using coded language. It's easy in a church setting to assume that everyone knows when "Advent" is or what "Communion preparation" means. A potential volunteer may nod politely as if understanding but in fact be totally in the dark. It's better to over-explain than assume comprehension.

- **Interviewers must be able to ask appropriate and meaningful questions.**

This takes practice to interview with grace, so plan to train your interviewers, even if they have strong people skills. In fact, *especially* if they have strong people skills.

Sometimes interviewers who love spending time with people tend to fill the first half of any interview time with chit-chat, sharing stories from their own lives. Establishing rapport is fine, but it can't take over an interview session. Nor can selling the potential volunteer on the wisdom of signing up to volunteer or reviewing facts that aren't really relevant until a potential volunteer is offered a position.

Some interview skills to sharpen in your volunteer team…

Ask open-ended questions, and make open-ended statements. An open-ended question or statement is one that can't be answered with a simple "yes" or "no" and usually reveals far more information than a directive, closed-ended question.

For instance, a closed-ended, directive question might be "Do you have a family?" You'll get an answer, but it might very well be just "yes" or "no." Instead, ask for family information in the form of an open-ended question or statement, such as "Tell me about your family." The answer will likely be something along the lines of "I have a husband and two children," followed by details.

One simple way to train your volunteers to use open-ended questions naturally is to have them form trios and practice on each other by assigning three roles: Interviewer, Interviewee, and Observer. Select a subject such as "My Last Vacation," and have the members of each trio take turns in the different roles.

Using open-ended questions is a habit your interviewers must form. And it *is* a habit—practice is essential.

Ask linking questions. A linking question is one that ties to something the person being interviewed has just said. It's an invitation to go deeper, to explain and explore more fully. A linking question communicates that the interviewer is actively listening, not just running down a list of questions and gathering the least amount of data needed.

Here's an example of linking questions following an open-ended statement:

Interviewer: *Tell me about your favorite volunteer experience.*

Potential Volunteer: *That would have to be when I was the Cub Scout leader for my son's Webelo pack. We had a great time together. I did that for two years.*

Interviewer: *What was it about being a pack leader that was so much fun?*

Potential Volunteer: *Part of it was being with my son and having that time with him. And part of it is that kids that age are just great. Lots of energy and creativity, and sometimes they even listened to me.*

Interviewer: *It sounds like you enjoy being with children.*

Potential Volunteer: *I love it. I was going to be a teacher but ended up not finishing college. In my last church, I got to teach in Sunday school, too.*

Interviewer: *But Cub Scouts was your favorite volunteer experience. I'm wondering why it ranked higher than teaching Sunday school.*

Potential Volunteer: *I think it's because the person running our Sunday school was so strict with the children. I had a hard time thinking it was so important they memorize a verse* *each week and that only the kids who did got treats. I didn't think that was fair to the kids who don't memorize well.*

See how much more information was revealed by using an open-ended approach and linking questions than by firing off a series of closed-ended questions? And yet the discussion wasn't confrontational or stilted. That natural flow comes with practice—help your interviewers get plenty of it.

- **Interviewers must use body language to make a connection.**

   The vast majority of communication is nonverbal, so train interviewers to maintain comfortable eye-contact with potential volunteers, and physically demonstrate they're listening by sitting in an open, attentive pose.

There are many, many resources to assist you in training interviewers to be more effective listeners, but the most effective one may be a member of your church or community who's a professional counselor. Most counselors have highly developed listening skills and could help your team become competent in those skills listed above. Invite such a person to sit down with you and plan a training session or two or to provide ongoing coaching.

A caution: Your interviewers are *not* counselors. They're not equipped to provide the care a trained counselor can provide. If you provide listening skills training, be clear about how to use those skills within the confines of the interview process. The goal of an interview isn't to do therapy; it's to gather appropriate information to determine where to refer the volunteer and to provide a listening ear. That's all. If something more is revealed and requires follow-up, train your interviewers in how to refer potential volunteers to a more qualified person.

"Your interviewers are *not* counselors."

A 90-minute training session is provided for you in the next chapter, beginning on page 87. It will increase the readiness of your volunteers to be effective listeners. You may also wish to have a training session to familiarize your interviewers with policies and procedures related to interviewing volunteers.

Develop Tools for Your Interviewers

Which tools you need depends on what process you use. We'd like to suggest a process for you to follow. It's one that's been used successfully in a variety of churches—large and small—and will be easy for you to adapt. It assumes you have trained interviewers, a system in place to capture and use information you gather, and people you can hand potential volunteers to for an additional interview and job offer.

This four-step process involves:

1. Sending a letter or e-mail to confirm interviews you have scheduled. (Include with the letter a Discovering My Abilities, Skills, and Passions form that interviewees will complete prior to their interviews.)

2. Conducting an interview using the Sample Interview Form as a guide.

3. Referring the potential volunteer to a ministry leader for a follow-up interview.

4. Confirming that the placement was successful.

The tools you will need are the confirmation letter, the Discovering My Abilities, Skills, and Passions form, an interview form, and a follow-up letter.

And good news—there are samples of these forms for your use at the end of this book!

Let's walk through the four steps...

1. Confirm the appointment.

Your marketing plan has been a success. People are interested in meeting with you or a member of your interview team to explore volunteering through the church.

It's helpful if potential volunteers give some thought to what they're good at doing before they arrive. They may be limiting their thinking about volunteering to only what they've done in church and, as a result, eliminating their ability to serve in an area of ability, skill, or passion.

The Reach Out—Renew—Rejoice letter on page 191 is an invitation to think more holistically and to prepare for a personal interview. Send the letter and a copy of the Discovering My Abilities, Skills, and Passions form on page 193 to each person you will interview about a week before the scheduled interview. That's enough time to thoughtfully, prayerfully consider the questions, but not so much time that people set aside the letter and form.

You may choose to underscore the importance of thinking about the questions presented in the letter and form by calling the person a few days before the appointment to confirm the time and place and to inquire if the letter and form arrived. Ask again that interviewees bring the completed form with them to their interviews.

There's a "hidden agenda" in making the confirmation call: It communicates that this is a serious appointment. Doctors' offices call to confirm appointments—you should, too.

2. Conduct the interview.

Here's where you and your team of interviewers put your training to use.

3. Refer the potential volunteer to a ministry leader for follow-up.

Assuming no red flag arose to indicate the potential volunteer should *not* serve as a volunteer, you'll now recommend one or more ministries in which the interviewee could serve.

Please remember that *you will not offer the interviewee a position*. It's up to the person who will supervise the interviewee to bring the volunteer on board. You'll be in a position to show the interviewee position descriptions and suggest placement…but that's all.

The moment you want to reach is the one where you present ministry opportunities and ask, "Does this appeal to you?" What drives the opportunities you present isn't a list of open positions; rather, it's which positions include abilities, talents, skills, and passions that align with those expressed by the interviewee.

The chart on page 85 summarizes how the interview process unfolds. It may be a handy tool to photocopy and place where you'll see it often.

4. Confirm that the placement was successful.

After suggesting a volunteer role for the interviewee, contact the person who supervises that position, and ask him or her to schedule a follow-up meeting with the person you or your team just interviewed. Then a week later, follow up again with that supervisor to see if an appointment has been set.

It's this step where too often the ball is dropped and potential volunteers lose heart that there's a place for them to serve. Even if there's no

> "Timing is everything."

current open position in the preschool ministry, if a potential volunteer expresses interest, the preschool director *must follow up promptly*. Timing is everything.

Also send the person you've interviewed an e-mail reminding him or her to expect a call for a follow-up interview. If a background check will be required for the desired position, say so in the e-mail. Again, that's not something to hide.

Three months after the placement has been made, schedule a follow-up meeting or phone call with both the supervisor and the volunteer. Find out how things are going and whether the placement is working. Seek to resolve any misunderstandings and conflicts. If a volunteer isn't thriving in his or her volunteer role, go through the interview process again and provide another, more appropriate, role.

There's another part of the volunteer placement that deserves a closer look: orientation. It's where you have the opportunity to ensure that volunteers get connected with the information and people they need to be successful.

You can't overestimate the need for outstanding volunteer orientation and training—and we'll be discussing these processes next.

Interview Process

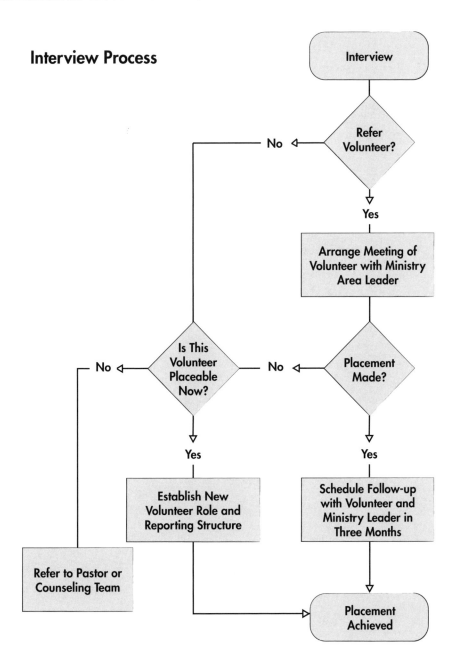

Interview

Refer Volunteer?

No

Yes

Arrange Meeting of Volunteer with Ministry Area Leader

Is This Volunteer Placeable Now?

No

Placement Made?

No

Yes

Yes

Establish New Volunteer Role and Reporting Structure

Schedule Follow-up with Volunteer and Ministry Leader in Three Months

Refer to Pastor or Counseling Team

Placement Achieved

Active Listening Training Workshop

A 90-minute workshop that will help you equip your team of interviewers.

In this hands-on workshop you will accomplish the following:

- Expose participants to five skills associated with active listening.

- Lead participants in practicing those five skills.

- Facilitate evaluation of participants in those five skills.

Supplies needed: Chairs, pens or pencils, a whiteboard or piece of posterboard and markers, one copy of the Active Listening Encouragement and Evaluation Sheet per participant (see end of this chapter), Bible, name tags.

Introduction

Welcome participants as they arrive. Even if you believe everyone knows the name of each other person, ask everyone to fill out a name tag. Have them write their first and last name and the name of a childhood pet, if they had a pet.

Encourage people to mingle and attempt to guess what sort of animal the other participants' pets were, based on the pets' names.

When the announced start time has arrived, gather participants together and say:

Welcome to this Active Listening Training Workshop. In the next 90 minutes we'll discover how the five skills associated with active listening can help us become better interviewers. We'll get a chance to practice those skills, too.

Let me admit right up front that all of us have room to grow in our listening skills—including me. This is a safe place to learn new things and to stumble a bit as we learn.

Open your Bible and read aloud 1 Peter 4:10, printed here for your convenience:

> "Each one should use whatever gift he has received to serve others, faithfully administering God's grace in its various forms" (1 Peter 4:10).

Say: **We can choose to become better interviewers for lots of reasons. It can be the challenge that intrigues us or that getting better at this will help us professionally. It's a valuable skill. Maybe it's because we're the sort of people who, if we do something, want to do it with excellence.**

Let me suggest this as a motivation: so we can cooperate with the purposes of God. It's clear in the passage I read and elsewhere in Scripture that each person in our church is designed by God to have a place in service. We're made to serve God in unique ways that we may not understand ourselves. The interviewing we'll do will help people find appropriate, rewarding places to serve. That makes what you do an important ministry!

And the skills you'll learn or have reinforced in this workshop are a big part of what will make you an effective interviewer.

Let's commit this time to God.

Lead in a prayer dedicating the workshop to God, and ask his blessing on your learning and application of what you're learning.

The Workshop

Say: **Listening is more than just waiting for your turn to speak. It's more than a way to gather information. When we truly listen, we communicate warmth that allows interviewees to open up and share what—and who—they really are. We help the people we're interviewing feel worthy and respected.**

Listening is a gift we give others.

In the next hour we'll identify and practice several techniques that help us actively listen to others. Active listening is simply this: listening to others and letting them know we're listening. Sounds simple, doesn't it?

It's not. Most listening is passive, not active. The two types of listening differ in some important ways:

- *Active* **listening requires us to be engaged and patient; passive listening demands nothing more than simply staying quiet.**

- *Active* **listening communicates concern, interest, and empathy; passive listening falls far short of that.**

- *Active* **listening often builds a relationship; passive listening usually doesn't.**

- **Finally,** *active* **listening is rare; passive listening isn't.**

Turn to a partner, and share about a time you talked with someone— maybe a friend or partner—and when you were done sharing, you felt truly heard. What was that like? You've got 2 minutes.

Allow 2 minutes, then call attention back to yourself by gently sounding a whistle or clapping.

Say: **Now share about a time when someone was hearing you but not really listening. What was that like? Again, you've got 2 minutes.**

Allow 2 more minutes; then call attention back to yourself again.

Say: **Quite a difference, wasn't there? Please call out a few words that describe how you felt when someone was** *truly* **listening to you—and let us know that. How did you feel?** Jot the descriptive words you hear on the whiteboard or piece of poster paper.

Now call out some words that describe how you felt when someone was not really listening. How did you feel? Jot the descriptive words you hear on the whiteboard or piece of poster paper.

Here's what's sad: If we talked to the people who were with us in our second situations—where someone was with us but not hearing us—those people would probably say they *were* **listening.**

Listening can be done well—or poorly. We're going to identify and practice some skills that make it likelier that someone we're interviewing will describe the experience with the *first* **list of words.**

Here's what we'll do: I'll briefly describe four active listening skills that we each need to master; then we'll get into teams and practice them. Please know that you don't need to become an expert in these to be effective. What you need is to listen to others in the way you want to be listened to; it's like the Golden Rule of Listening.

Here are the skills...

Skill #1: Help the interviewee feel comfortable.

Some of this is what you do physically. (Demonstrate as you continue.) **For instance, be sure you place chairs so there's no barrier between you, but don't have chairs face-to-face—that's confrontational. Sit at a slight angle so you can talk comfortably. Sit up straight, leaning slightly forward so you appear attentive and focused. Maintain eye contact that's comfortable, but not a stare-down. And minimize distractions by turning off your cell phone and any radio or television that might snag your attention or the attention of the interviewee.**

Also, speak in a pleasant, relaxed tone. Don't rush through your questions or speak loudly.

Skill #2: Communicate that you're listening.

React to what you're being told by nodding, raising your eyebrows, or responding in another nonverbal way to the emotion and content you're hearing. The idea isn't to become a mime, but to provide clues that you're attentive and listening carefully.

Occasionally saying something like "I see" or "uh-huh" will provide verbal clues you're listening, too, but use them sparingly.

One great way to communicate you're listening is to use linking questions and provide an opportunity for the interviewee to elaborate.

Skill #3: Focus on what you're hearing.

Listening is *hard work*. It requires us to do things we don't normally do...

- *Keep an open mind.* It's hard to wait until the interviewee is finished talking before you decide if you agree or disagree or form an opinion. We often listen just long enough to reach a conclusion and then express ourselves. The problem with this approach is that an interviewee may not know what she thinks about something until she's done sharing. And *we* certainly don't know. We must keep an open mind.

- *Focus only on the speaker.* Try to avoid thinking about what you're going to say next or about your own concerns. You can't be thinking about whether you rolled up your car windows and what an interviewee is saying at the same time.

- *Don't do too much sharing.* It may seem odd to say, but although you're trying to develop a relationship, it is usually counterproductive to disclose too much about yourself. The purpose of the interview isn't for you to share your volunteer experiences, but to draw out the interviewee. Disclose who you are but only as it encourages the interviewee to share. If the interviewee asks you questions about yourself, respond—but redirect the interview back to the person being interviewed.

Skill #4: Reflect back what you hear.

This is perhaps the most difficult skill to master. You want to be able to reflect what you've heard by paraphrasing what you've been told. This allows you to know if you've listened accurately and to give the interviewee the chance to correct you.

Here's what's tricky: You need to reflect *both* parts of the message you've received—the content and the emotion.

Here's an example of something you might hear from Mary when you're interviewing her: "When I was a volunteer at First Church, it was a good experience." (Deliver this line calmly and in a straightforward manner.)

Pretty straightforward, right? You might paraphrase that remark by saying, "Sounds like when you were at First Church you enjoyed being a volunteer."

Notice that my reflection paraphrase sums up both the *content* of what she *said*—she was a volunteer at First Church—and what I understood that she *felt* about being a volunteer—she enjoyed it. She never said she enjoyed it, she implied she enjoyed it. I put a word in her mouth to make sure I'm clear about how she felt.

If I was right, Mary might say, "Oh, yes, I loved getting together with the other volunteers, and we became friends. I hope the same thing happens here." That's some valuable information about what motivates Mary to volunteer.

If I was wrong about how she felt, Mary will correct me. She might say, "No, I really hated it. It was good because it helped me be less shy, but I couldn't stand the people I was with." That's helpful to know, too!

Think of each message you receive as having two parts: content and emotion. Sometimes the content is really big and there's hardly any emotion. A lecture about cellular biology in science class is usually like that. The teacher sends you tons of content, but it isn't that emotional.

Other times a message has very little content, but lots of emotion. When you tell someone you want to marry "I love you" for the first time, there's not much content—but a *lot* of emotion.

When you reflect back to people what you're hearing, reflect both content and emotion. That can be tough because we're used to thinking we "get it" when people tell us things, that we don't have any cause to check if our assumptions are correct.

That's dangerous. Communication is so complex that it's amazing we ever understand each other at all. And where we misunderstand each other is often about how we feel. If you tell me your grandmother died, it means something very different if she was a big part of your life than if she was someone you'd never met who refused to see you. The content is the same, the emotion completely different.

So what happens if you reflect to someone that you think they're sad, when they're not? They're really angry, but they look sad.

Here's what happens: They correct you and move on. As long as your reflection is tentative, nonjudgmental, and it's obvious you want to understand, people don't hold it against you that you read them wrong. They straighten you out and move on.

How do you reflect? Here's a simple formula you can use until the process feels more natural and you can substitute wording of your own:

"Let me be sure I understand. You were a volunteer at your former church (there's the content), and you feel good about the experience (there's the emotion)."

And if you're stuck for a word that sums up the emotion, consider using one of these words: *mad, sad, glad,* or *scared.* They pretty much capture everything someone can feel.

See how challenging active listening can be? You need to listen not just to the words but also to the emotions. You have to focus. You try not to jump in or make judgments, and you want to encourage someone else to keep talking. It's hard!

Let's practice some of those skills right now. Believe it or not, it's fun—and you'll see huge improvement in your skills as you practice.

Form trios, and ask the person in each trio who has the next birthday to be the Interviewer. The person with the next birthday after that will be the Interviewee. The last person in each trio will be the Observer. Trios will need to sit far enough apart from other trios that conversations can happen easily, but it will be helpful if you can see each trio. That will help you signal stop times and let you see if a trio gets stuck.

Ask the Interviewer to arrange the chairs so they're angled and it's comfortable to talk. The Observer should sit off to one side where he or she can hear but won't be in the direct line of vision. Give the Observer a copy of the Active Listening Encouragement and Evaluation Sheet (found at the end of this chapter) and a pencil or pen. Tell participants they'll interview for 8 minutes, but they don't need to watch the clock; you'll interrupt to call the session to a close. Encourage the Observer to take notes of times they see examples of what's on the sheet. And be specific—the more specific the feedback, the more helpful it is.

You'll have six rounds of interviews, and you need to provide topics that elicit both content and emotion but don't turn into deeper sessions than your trios are prepared to handle. Use one of these topics, or develop your own:

- Describe a family vacation from your youth.

- Describe a time from your childhood when you struggled in school.

- Describe a time in your life you were frightened.

- Describe a time you took on a challenge and were successful.

- Describe something you'd change about your house or apartment if you could.

- Describe something you'd do if you had 50 million dollars.

Once you've announced the topic and given the interviewee 30 seconds to think about it, start the interviews. Expect a lot of nervous laughter the first few times you have practice sessions; you're pulling people out of their comfort zones.

At the 5-minute mark, blow a whistle gently or clap your hands. Ask everyone to take a deep breath, stretch their muscles, and then move the chairs so both the Interviewer and Interviewee face the Observer. Then ask the Observer to go through the Encouragement and Evaluation Sheet and give examples of what the Interviewer did well. The sheet also directs the Observer to ask the Interviewer and Interviewee how the process felt. Allow time for this discussion; then quickly move on.

Ask members of each trio to rotate chairs and do the exercise again with a new topic. Each member of the trio will have each role once. The way trios decide who goes next is up to them.

After you've participated in three interviews, tell participants they'll do another three interviews in round-robin fashion, with one change: Observers will now also take notes on how the Interviewer can improve. Instead of just encouragement, there will also be critique and evaluation. The goal will be to help Interviewers identify what skills they need to practice in the context of additional conversations at home or work.

You Should Be in Pictures

A Note: If you have the technology or you are working with a very small group, another way to provide feedback is to videotape each session and include the Interviewer in viewing the tape. Nothing shows us more clearly how we're actually behaving than a video of ourselves. Interviewers will tend to see only their shortcomings, so be careful to be especially affirming.

After the second round of interviews, gather participants together. Ask participants how they feel about their practice sessions and how they'll put the four active learning skills to use elsewhere in their lives.

Suggest each participant take an Active Listening Encouragement and Evaluation Sheet home to keep handy. If you intend to hold another training or orientation session regarding procedures and policies, announce it at this point.

Active Listening Encouragement and Evaluation Sheet

As you observe the interview, make notes about the following interview skills. Your candid feedback will help the Interviewer grow in ministry effectiveness. Remember to be specific in your feedback and to offer compliments as well as critique.

Helps the Interviewee feel comfortable.

☐ Removes physical barriers to conversation.
☐ Sits up straight or leans slightly forward.
☐ Makes consistent eye contact.
☐ Speaks in pleasant, relaxed tone.
☐ Doesn't appear to be distracted or rushed.

Communicates listening.

☐ Is physically responsive with nods or facial movements.
☐ Provides sparing verbal cues.
☐ Uses open-ended questions.
☐ Uses linking questions.

Focuses on Interviewee.

☐ Displays nonjudgmental attitude.
☐ Displays patience.
☐ Appropriately self-disclosing.

Reflects back what Interviewee communicates.

☐ Paraphrases content.
☐ Paraphrases emotion.

After giving your feedback, ask both the Interviewer and Interviewee how they felt about the interview. What feedback does the Interviewee have for the Interviewer? What does the Interviewer think are his or her strengths…and weaknesses?

Orientation Defined

Orientation is a process, not a one-shot program. Here's how to create a process that meets the needs of your volunteers—and your paid ministry staff, too.

For years you've entered your name in contests, filling out little cards and sending in box tops for drawings, and for years your name has never been drawn—until now.

The knock on your door was official notification that you're the Grand Prize Winner, and your all-expenses-paid trip to Italy will begin immediately. You've got just enough time to stuff two suitcases full of the clothes you think you'll need for your week in beautiful Tuscany, where you'll stay at a private villa.

Within an hour, you're whisked away by limousine to the airport, where a chartered jet wings you away on your whirlwind journey.

On the way, you use the complimentary phone to call everyone you can think of: family, friends, even people you hardly know. A private secretary is at your house, cleaning, filling the dishwasher, and phoning the Curl Up & Dye Hair Salon to cancel your appointment since Giuliano (who coifs all the Italian movie stars) will visit the villa to give you a complete makeover.

The jet lands, and you're given your choice of any rental car you want, including the sporty red convertible you've long wished you could afford back home. You hop in, a map spread out on the

> "You're soon winding your way through the rolling hills of Tuscany."

seat beside you, and with the radio blaring opera, you're soon winding your way through the rolling hills of Tuscany, the landscape lush with vineyards, olive trees, and cypress groves.

Unfortunately, as you approach a medieval town carved into a hillside, you find the road growing narrow—too narrow for your car. Your villa, unfortunately, rests high above the town on a rocky outcrop. There's no way to reach the villa except through the town's center, where cobbled streets were designed for horses, not horsepower. You should have taken a scooter instead of a car.

You schlep your suitcases up through town, smiling and nodding as you go. This is the Tuscany of your dreams, but it's also the Tuscany that's off the beaten tourist path. Few people can give you directions in English, so your search for the specific road that will take you to the villa is long, torturous, and extremely uphill.

You no sooner reach the villa (the view is *magnifico,* by the way) when you toss your laptop on the marble desktop. You dig the adaptor you bought when you were hoping to visit another country someday out of your computer case, plug it in, and immediately fry your computer. Nobody told you that household current is 220 volts in Italy, not the 110 your trusty laptop was wired to lovingly accept. You won't be e-mailing home to tell people about the wonderful time you're having.

Nor will you be doing much walking through the charming town, as you brought sandals and you're already feeling blisters form. You had no idea that the main form of transportation in this town was walking.

So sitting in Tuscany, in a villa that would be right at home in *Italian Dream Vacations* magazine, you stamp your foot (which pops a blister) and shout, "Why didn't someone tell me about this place?"

What you needed—and didn't get—was an orientation.

When you don't have enough information about an environment where you'll spend time—even wonderful Tuscany—the experience can be horrible. You're unprepared for the terrain. You don't know what to expect from the people you'll meet. You don't know the culture, how to accomplish things, or who to call for help. You feel alone and vulnerable.

And to a volunteer walking into a junior high boys Sunday school class for the first time, that's exactly how it feels.

You've invested a great deal of time and energy in finding, interviewing, and placing volunteers. If you fail to orient those volunteers into your ministry and their unique roles in it, you may well undo all you've accomplished.

There's tremendous power in a well-run orientation process. Not only can it salvage a Tuscan vacation, it can also keep your volunteers happy and on board.

The Power and Benefits of an Orientation Process

Notice that orientation is being referred to as a *process,* not just a *program.* That's because to be effective, an orientation will take more than a one-shot program—even if that program stretches over several days.

Remember, an orientation answers the question "What's life like around here?" That's not a question that can usually be answered quickly or in one session. It's something a new volunteer discovers over the course of time.

> " An orientation answers the question, 'What's life like around here?' "

You can help that discovery process along, and in this chapter, we'll tell you how. It's good to have a formal orientation program as a kickoff, but don't make the mistake of thinking that will be enough. It won't, at least for most volunteers.

The nuts and bolts of a volunteer's position are described on his or her ministry description...but position descriptions tell new volunteers what they'll be doing, not what life is like. Position descriptions leave lots of questions unanswered, such as...

- "Where's the closest bathroom?"

- "If I leave my lunch in the church refrigerator, will someone steal it?"

- "Is it okay to tell jokes and laugh around here?"

Deliver a great orientation for your volunteers, and you'll answer their questions. You'll put them at ease. And...

- **You'll reassure volunteers they made a good decision in volunteering.**

  If the orientation is positive and helpful, it reinforces the volunteer's decision to be involved. It's not the first impression your volunteer ministry has made, but it's the first significant taste of the actual position. In a world where promises are often made ("You'll enjoy this volunteer role—sign up and find out for yourself!") and then broken, your follow-up will be noticeable and appreciated.

  Scott, a volunteer in an Indiana church, describes his first volunteer role at the church he attended: "I was asked by a ministry leader to direct the Wednesday evening children's program for a period of three months. I checked to make sure my schedule was clear, then jumped on the opportunity.

  "After I accepted, the ministry leader looked at me, patted me on the back, and said, 'I'm so sorry. Good luck.'

  "That leader didn't reassure me at all. Basically he told me I'd made a mistake by taking the bait, that I'd soon regret it, and that heading up that program was the most difficult thing I'd ever do."

  Fortunately, Scott immediately recruited a few close friends to help him with the program, and the three months were a blast for the leaders and the kids. But if Scott hadn't been the enthusiastic guy he is, he could easily have quit before he ever reached his first Wednesday night.

- **You'll connect the volunteer ministry position to the larger purpose of the church.**

  Here's your chance to cement in a volunteer's mind how his or her position contributes to the larger mission of the church.

  There are a dozen versions of a story that communicates this concept well. Here's one version you can share with your volunteers. Consider including it in your orientation programs to help volunteers catch a vision for how every position is important and contributes to the cause. One manager gives each new person on his team a copy of this story and a cobblestone to use as a paperweight.

During the middle ages, a Swiss bishop made the long journey to Germany to see the Frankfurt Cathedral. Still under construction after a hundred years, the cathedral would someday be the largest in Europe, a magnificent monument to God. A place where thousands would gather and worship.

The portly cleric rode through mountain passes into Germany. Miles from Frankfurt, the bishop could see the unfinished cathedral towering over the town, an enormous skeleton of supports and timbers. Massive gray walls rose where stone masons slowly fitted together row after row of huge blocks.

Eventually, the bishop stood in the very shadow of the cathedral. Around him swarmed an army of engineers, stone cutters, and carpenters. Crew chiefs shouted orders, pulleys creaked as stones were pushed and pulled into position, and the pounding of chisels and hammers echoed off soaring walls.

The bishop touched the arm of a man hurrying past. "Tell me what you're doing," the bishop said.

"I've got to recalculate the angle of the nave roof before we all get crushed," snapped the man. "Step aside!" And with that the man huffed away.

The bishop noticed a half dozen laborers holding a rope that wound up into the distant darkness above, then back down where it was tied around a large stone block.

"What are you doing?" asked the bishop.

The workers exchanged annoyed glances. "Well, Father," said one, "we're hoisting this block up to the top—unless you can talk God into floating it there." The men laughed, squared their grip on the thick rope, then leaned into their back-breaking task.

The bishop saw a small, elderly man sitting near a doorway. He was hunched over, chiseling cobblestones. The bishop's heart went out to the man—obviously a stonemason whose age and failing eyesight made him good for nothing but this thankless task. A craftsman whose life had been reduced to chiseling stones for a walkway in some forgotten corner.

"And you," said the bishop. "Tell me what you're doing."

The old man looked up without missing a beat. "Me? I'm doing the same as everyone else—to God's glory, I'm building a cathedral."

A well-crafted orientation program helps volunteers see the importance of what they're doing. It's an opportunity for them to discover how their roles serve God, advance the work of the church, and have eternal significance.

- **You'll reduce volunteer turnover.**

  There's a direct correlation between orientation and retention. You've placed volunteers where their abilities, skills, and passions connect with a volunteer role, but they're not yet at home in that role. During their orientation, you'll help them feel comfortable—and a volunteer who's comfortable, challenged, and growing is one who's likely to stick.

  On the other hand, if a volunteer feels unwelcome—for any reason— that volunteer isn't likely to be with you long.

- **You'll help volunteers be successful in two ways—culture and information.**

  Matching a volunteer with the right position is only part of what sets a person up for success. The volunteer also has to match up with the culture where he or she is serving and master the information that's required for him or her to be successful.

  Let's start by considering what happens when the culture of the volunteer collides with the culture of the ministry area.

Connecting With Culture:
Jackie and the Whoopee Cushion

Jackie is a quiet, serious musician who wants to join her church's music ministry. She's sung in choirs since she was a girl, and she has a high regard for the dignity and majesty of choral music. Her choir experience has always been in choirs that prepared thoroughly and performed complicated choral pieces brilliantly.

She's gifted, skilled, and eager to sign on as a volunteer vocalist. To Jackie, serving in this spot seems like a match made in heaven. She can't wait for the first practice session.

Except the church's approach to music ministry is to lead worship, not to perform. And the music team isn't all that worried about hitting every note perfectly or choosing challenging choral pieces. By intent, the group selects easy-to-sing worship choruses and plays in an accessible, simple way so everyone can join in.

Plus, it's a tight-knit group that has fun as well as does ministry. During Jackie's first practice session, the bass player leaves a whoopee cushion under the pad on the piano stool. The loud "pffffffffft" that echoes around the sanctuary when the keyboard player sits down prompts so much laughter that even the music director is howling hysterically.

What are the odds that Jackie will last as a member of the music ministry? that she'll even survive her first night of practice with the team?

> ## What are the odds that Jackie will last?

In spite of her many musical gifts, there's a total disconnect when it comes to culture. In Jackie's case, the distance might be so great that nothing could help her bridge the gap—but an orientation would be helpful. And it might be enough.

At the very least, an orientation to the music ministry and its culture would keep Jackie from being scandalized and angry.

Granted, Jackie's case is extreme. But even for people who don't have to figure out how to transition from the Mormon Tabernacle Choir to the Mostly Tentative Choir, culture can be a problem.

> "Orientation is where you cover culture."

And it's a problem you can solve by taking volunteers through an orientation. Orientation is where you cover culture—and help volunteers decide how they'll fit in. You'll give new volunteers the understanding and tools they need to effectively enter into new roles, surrounded by new people, working on new teams.

You can't overstate the impact of culture on a volunteer's experience. If volunteers don't understand the church culture or embrace the values of your ministry, they'll never feel at home.

But how do you communicate culture?

Church Culture Components

Let's answer that question by first examining what components combine to create our culture at church and in our ministry.

Information—How is it distributed? Is it widely shared, or does confidentiality play a role that must be respected? How does a volunteer go about learning things?

Technology—How highly regarded is the latest technology? What does a volunteer need to know—and why?

Power—Who's in charge? What's their style of sharing—or not sharing—power? How is power expressed? What are volunteers allowed to decide on their own? For what must they seek approval, and from whom?

Economics—How is money viewed in the ministry? What's scarce and must be used carefully, and what seems to be always available in abundance? How do people go about getting what they need?

Values—What does the ministry hold in high regard? What does it believe? How are those beliefs expressed? How thoroughly are the values integrated in the culture—is everyone on board? How clear are the preferred values?

Tradition—What traditions are part of how things are done? Who's the keeper of the flame for the traditions? Are the traditions embraced, tolerated, or somewhere in between? How are the traditions celebrated?

Rules and regulations—What are the rules that maintain order in the culture? How are those rules structured? What are the penalties for breaking the rules?

Tone—What's the emotional tone of the culture? Is it okay to have fun? How much fun? How do people have fun? Are there times the culture demands solemnity? When and why?

Change—How open is the culture to changing things? What sort of things are changeable, and which are "sacred cows" that seem immune to change? How does one go about instigating change?

Pecking order—Who's important and who's less important? How is that demonstrated? How are segments of people divided—and why?

Who is "the enemy"?—Is there a cause that the culture seeks to promote or a group or cause that has been identified as the enemy? What cause will encourage the culture to circle the wagons or send out the sentries?

Watering holes—Where does the culture gather for support and sustenance? Where is the culture in evidence and celebrated?

Acclimating to a new culture is an ongoing process. Allow time and opportunity for it to happen. It's simply not possible to work through a list of cultural elements like those listed above in one brief meeting.

> "Acclimating to a new culture is an ongoing process."

And a word of caution: You might think that because someone was raised in your church and already knows the people with whom he or she will be serving, there's no need for an orientation. You would be wrong. There's a huge difference between being a student in a class and teaching the class. And what's valued in the high school youth group will vary dramatically from what's valued in the preschool ministry.

In addition to covering culture, orientations will help volunteers in another way…

Connecting With Information: Mrs. Brown and the Missing Envelopes

Orientation is also where you can shorten the learning curve for volunteers. You can tell them what they need to know instead of hoping they'll figure it out on their own…something that may never happen.

At one church, the Sunday school superintendent received a complaint from the offering usher about Mrs. Brown, a Sunday school teacher who failed to turn in the offering collected in her second grade classroom. Other teachers placed the change they collected in envelopes, then slid the envelopes under their classroom doors. The designated offering usher went down the hallway collecting envelopes while classes were underway.

There was never an envelope outside Mrs. Brown's door.

Theories were floated. Was she pocketing the estimated two dollars in change each Sunday? spending it on classroom supplies? failing to take an offering at all? What could be done? What should be done? Did the pastor know?

Finally, the supervisor asked Mrs. Brown about the class offering. She replied that no one had ever told her about any envelope procedure. She'd been collecting the money in Sunday school, then dropping it in the offering plate an hour later when a collection was taken during church.

Mrs. Brown had circumvented the offering envelope procedure but still accomplished the goal: Offering money was collected and turned in. Once the process was explained, without fail an envelope scooted out from under her door each Sunday. Satisfied, the offering usher declared Mrs. Brown a success.

Volunteer Orientation Objectives

What information you share in an orientation meeting depends on what you want to accomplish. Do you have a clear purpose and set of objectives? Without them, you don't have much chance of having a meaningful orientation meeting. Nor will you know if you were effective in meeting your objectives.

> "What information you share depends on what you want to accomplish."

Whatever you settle on as objectives for your orientation process, be sure you're hitting them by measuring results. It may be a year or more before you have enough volunteers entering or leaving the program to be able to determine impact, but it's important to begin now. The sooner you start, the sooner you'll know how to tweak volunteer orientations so you're making the most of the program.

If your objective was to transmit information, administer a test to be sure volunteers are learning and retaining the information.

If your objective was to reduce volunteer turnover, track whether volunteers exposed to the orientation program stayed longer than other volunteers.

If your objective was to help volunteers become effective sooner, do interviews with volunteers six weeks into their volunteer experience. Ask how what they covered in orientation helped—or hindered—their ability to master their jobs.

Whatever your objectives, it's likely you'll be sharing information at orientation meetings. Since that's a given, be careful about selecting what information you'll include. Ask yourself and, perhaps, your task force:

- *What information has proven to be most useful to new volunteers?*

- *Who is best suited to present the information?*

- *When is the information most appropriately presented?*

- *What logistical information do new volunteers need?*

> As you answer these questions, three things will quickly become obvious.

- *What problems and challenges are typically encountered by new volunteers?*

- *What policies and procedures do new volunteers need to know?*

As you answer these questions, three things will quickly become obvious...

- **Not every volunteer needs precisely the same information.**

  For instance, a Sunday morning greeter might need a far more detailed awareness of how the building is laid out than the volunteer who's in charge of mowing the yard.

  This reality suggests that some orientation is task specific and needs to be done later, when the entire group isn't assembled. To force a bus driver to sit through a discussion about the proper cleaning of the communion cups is a waste of time—and guarantees the bus driver won't be back for more meetings.

- **There is some information every volunteer needs.**

  Where to park, what standards of conduct are expected, where the first aid kit is located—that's information that's universally needed.

  This reality suggests that truly universal information is so important that it needs to be written down and accessible. A volunteer handbook and volunteer website are two good places for this information to reside even after an orientation meeting.

- **There's some information you may not have.**

  You may have suspicions about what problems are most often encountered by new volunteers, but do you really know? You probably only hear about a fraction of the challenges faced by new volunteers; you're guessing about the rest.

  This reality suggests that if you want to have a relevant orientation, you need to be asking volunteers to recommend what to include in the orientation. A survey of both current and new volunteers will provide agenda items.

And be sure that paid and unpaid staff who supervise volunteers have input, too. You want the orientation to meet their needs as well as the needs of the volunteers.

Whatever else your orientation covers, these items are generally a good idea to include:

- **The organizational chart (with no names listed next to titles)**
- **The church history, vision statement, and mission statement**
- **Your ministry's history, vision statement, and mission statement**
- **Training opportunities—who, what, when, where, why, and how**
- **Performance expectations and appraisal**
- **Safety information—evacuation plans, severe storm plans, and first aid kit location**
- **Logistics—where to park, where to find the coffee pot, etc.**
- **In every orientation meeting, be open for questions, comments, and observations from volunteers. Volunteers are absorbing information and assimilating into the culture; provide every opportunity for them to ask questions and get answers.**

No matter what content you include, the initial meeting should be brief, relevant, and direct. Especially if you want volunteers to be back for more orientation or ongoing training meetings, demonstrate that you can run a purposeful meeting that doesn't drag on forever.

The First Volunteer Orientation Meeting

There's often a formal orientation event for new volunteers, an initial meeting where general information is shared and administrative matters are addressed. This has great value, as it helps volunteers assimilate quickly and easily.

But that initial event often results in a severe case of information overload. The new volunteer is inundated with details that can't possibly all be absorbed. Eyes glaze over. People fidget. So much data is pushed at volunteers that it's amazing any of it is retained at all.

> **Provide the right information at the right time.**

A better solution is to give new volunteers less information, but to come back to talk with them several times. An initial meeting is worthwhile, but to avoid overload, be careful to provide the right information at the right time.

At your initial meeting be certain to:

- Warmly, sincerely welcome new volunteers, and ease their transition into new volunteer roles.

- Communicate essential information—but only essential information.

- Remind volunteers of the ministry's expectations about their conduct and contributions.

- Distribute and review any orientation handbooks that are needed by volunteers.

- Offer to answer general questions that are of interest to everyone present. If a question is job-specific, respond to the interested volunteer after the meeting, or refer the volunteer to his or her ministry supervisor.

That's all you need to do at an initial, formal orientation meeting.

Is there more information volunteers need to know? Absolutely—but in a one-shot, group setting that's probably all anyone can take in. The rest of the material you can cover later in smaller groups organized around volunteer assignments, or in a one-on-one setting.

The fact is that at an orientation meeting volunteers probably don't yet know what they need to know. They won't have a clear picture of what's truly important information to master until they dive into their roles and hit a few snags.

Remember the trip you won to Tuscany? You didn't know what you needed to know about Italian electrical current until you'd toasted your computer or that walking is the standard mode of travel in small Tuscan villages until your toes were blistered and sore.

You learned from experience—and in some ways you want your orientation program to save your volunteers from a similar fate. Some things are great to learn from experience...but why make the same mistakes others have made?

Jim Wideman, a children's pastor who has more than a thousand volunteers involved in his program, says it well: "Experience is the best teacher...but it doesn't have to be *your* experience."

The secret of an effective orientation program doesn't lie in hosting a tremendous formal meeting anyway. It's this: Effective orientation is an ongoing process. You can't hold one orientation meeting and then cross it off your list forever.

> "Effective orientation is an ongoing process."

Remember, the purpose of orientation is to answer the question "What's it like to live or work here?" Every time a volunteer changes jobs or the job the volunteer is doing changes or the culture or rules change—it's time for more orientation. The process never actually stops. Never.

Who Should Lead the Orientation Program and Process?

At the risk of sounding ungrateful, let us suggest that you may not be the best candidate for the job.

Not that you haven't done great work in connecting the new volunteers with appropriate service opportunities. And not that you wouldn't do a stellar job of facilitating the orientation. After all, you're probably the one who pulled the information together.

But you probably aren't the person who will be supervising the volunteers or being in a primary relationship with them. If you have enough volunteers entering into a particular area of ministry, it's a good idea to let the person who will be supervising them do the orientation.

Of course, maybe the new crop of volunteers will report to you or your volunteer ministry is small enough that you can be in relationship with everyone. If that's the case, go to it. Lead the orientation program yourself—but still involve others in the overall process.

> Have people who will be working with the volunteers attend the formal orientation.

And have the people who will be working with the volunteers attend the formal orientation. From the very start, you can help volunteers find buddies who know the ropes, who serve in the ministry roles in which the new volunteers will serve.

A Case Study: The Group Mission Trips Orientation Program

Each summer, Group Mission Trips organizes more than 100 week-long short-term mission programs where teenagers repair homes of the elderly and disadvantaged. The vast majority of the leaders at those Workcamps—each of which is housed in a community school and involves an average of 350 teenagers and youth leaders—are volunteers.

More than a thousand volunteers are needed each summer, and because of the program's reputation and excellence, each year that number of volunteers is recruited, screened, placed, and trained. Workcamp volunteers do everything from manage the school kitchens, to coordinate travel, to work alongside teenagers as together they roof a house or paint a porch.

Note the scope of this volunteer program—it's huge. The Workcamps themselves are scattered in communities all over the continent. There are more than a dozen volunteer roles at each camp, and one of the more challenging is the job of director.

Directors are the people ultimately responsible for running the Workcamps. If a youth leader falls through a ceiling or the food vendor fails to deliver the lettuce or a teenager drifts away from a worksite, the director gets involved.

Because of the complexity of preparing for the role, there's an orientation for Workcamp directors in Colorado each May. Volunteers who will direct camps are flown in, housed at the YMCA in the Rockies, and given three days of orientation and training.

And during those three days, what do you think is the single most energetically received session?

It's this: a several-hour meeting where new directors get the opportunity to ask veteran directors what to expect. There's no agenda other than to connect first-time volunteers with people who've dealt with the same responsibilities before.

The orientation is relational, not agenda-driven, and relationships that form continue through e-mails, text messages, phone calls, and encouraging notes between peers. The session sets an expectation that directors will be helpful to each other and responsive when there's a question or concern.

> The orientation is relational, not agenda-driven.

The 3-inch-thick orientation and training manual every director receives is packed with helpful information. It's useful. It's referred to often. It's practical and well organized.

But the manual isn't the magic.

Something else happens during that three-day orientation and training meeting that shapes volunteers into directors who will embrace a week-long Workcamp experience that keeps them up into the wee hours of the morning day after day. That requires them to be servants even if they're tired. That inspires them to deliver top-flight customer service to teenagers and youth leaders alike.

Here's what happens during those three days that makes the difference— and you can reap similar rewards if you can build these elements into your orientation program, too…

- **Volunteers are immersed in Workcamp culture.**

   The staff hosting the orientation doesn't just talk about serving others; they model it in a hundred ways to the new volunteers. Meetings start and end promptly. Questions are answered clearly. Requested information is tracked down and reported. The needs of volunteers are taken seriously—which is exactly what will be expected of the directors when they're running their own camps.

   For three solid days, the Group Mission Trips vision, mission, and values are soaked up by volunteers.

   Anything that will be expected of directors at their Workcamps is modeled during the orientation. That way there's never a question as to what's meant by "service" or "leadership." Everyone has experienced it.

- **Top people lead the orientation program.**

   When the senior pastor or CEO shows up to lead an orientation session, that communicates the significance of the orientation process. At the Group Mission Trips orientation new volunteers hear from—and have dinner with—the founder of the program. And the people leading sessions are front-line staff.

   Be sure you have your best people leading your orientation programs, too. And having your senior pastor show up to personally thank your volunteers for their commitment and servant hearts will fire up your team.

- **Stories are shared.**

There's power in stories. The stories we share carry the DNA of our values and culture. The stories highlight what's important and lift up heroes to emulate.

> **There's power in stories.**

At the Group Mission Trips orientation, stories play a central role. They're told to illustrate what works—and doesn't work. What's wise—and what's foolish. What matters—and what's not important. Stories are shared with humor and laughter, but never is the point missed: There's truth in these stories. Let those with ears hear and understand.

In your orientation process, tell the story of how your volunteer ministry came into being. In the process, you'll share what vision motivated your founders to persevere until the ministry was born. Tell stories about volunteers who've made you proud—they embody the attributes that are considered virtues in your culture.

And never miss the opportunity to capture stories as they unfold in your ministry. The best stories you could tell next year may well be happening right now.

- **New volunteers are celebrated.**

There's always a temptation for veterans to form cliques. It's just natural: They're friends who've shared experiences, and perhaps they seldom see each other between annual orientation sessions.

Although it's natural, it's toxic for new volunteers.

At the Group Mission Trips orientation, newcomers are intentionally integrated into sessions with veteran volunteers. Past experience is applauded and appreciated, but in many ways it's irrelevant. The focus is preparing for the summer ahead, not reminiscing about past Workcamps. New volunteers are given high honor for their willingness to serve and celebrated as legitimate members of the team.

How do you handle cliques among your volunteers—especially among groups of long-term volunteers? Where is there an opportunity for newcomers to be heard, accepted, and endorsed?

- **Evaluations are filled out.**

  How do you know what's effective in preparing your volunteers for their roles and what's not helping? You ask your volunteers. They know—at least, the experienced volunteers know.

  Don't let a formal orientation program in your church go past without designing in an evaluation of the program and the process. For your convenience, a Program Evaluation Form is on page 198. Adapt it to use at your formal orientation programs. You'll also be asking volunteers to fill out the same form after three to six months; comparing their answers will let you know what they remember and what was most and least helpful.

  You probably won't be flying your volunteers to a remote mountain getaway for three days anytime soon. But you can pull together a one-day retreat...or even a half-day retreat. It's a chance for you to transform volunteers into servants who will rise above even their own expectations.

6 The Volunteer Orientation Staff Handbook

Most organizations provide a handbook to staff members during orientation—and you should, too. Here's why...and what you need to include.

Denise's first day at her new job wasn't quite what she expected.

"First we had a tour of the facility," she reports. "I saw where I'd be sitting and figured out where to hang my coat and stash my purse. I had lunch with one of the people on my team. That stuff I pretty much knew was coming."

What took Denise by surprise was how she spent the afternoon.

"Six of us sat in a little conference room for three hours," she says in amazement. "We opened up an employee handbook and took turns reading through it—out loud. Then we had to sign a form that said we'd read the handbook. I was bored out of my mind."

Denise shakes her head as she remembers what felt like a wasted afternoon. "I just can't believe that was the best use of our time. We had a million things we could have done, and they had us reading out loud like we were in first grade. Somebody must really care about that handbook," she says.

It probably was the best use of Denise's time to read through the handbook. While the presentation style was at best mind-numbing, it did expose Denise and the other new hires to critical information they need to know.

And because everyone walked out of the conference room with a copy of the handbook, Denise knows where to find the details she's forgotten when she's wondering how to schedule vacation time or wondering what the company's policy is about snow days.

But that's a for-profit company. They need orientation handbooks for new hires, right? Does your volunteer ministry really require you to create one?

Yes…and here's why.

Five Reasons You Need a Volunteer Ministry Orientation Handbook

Creating a handbook can be a time-consuming task, even if you start with another church's handbook as a model. But without question developing a handbook is worth the investment—for at least five reasons.

1. Orientation handbooks compensate for information overload.

Volunteers can absorb just so much information at a time. Trying to cram too many policies and procedures into their heads at one time is like continuing to pour milk into a glass that's already full: There's no more room.

> A handbook provides the details in a handy reference guide.

A handbook provides the details in a handy reference guide. The volunteer may not recall exactly what the policy is about appropriate clothing, but she knows where to look it up.

2. Orientation handbooks are open 24/7.

Who are the volunteers going to call if they can't remember the procedure for lining up a substitute Sunday school teacher? You—of course. Do you really want that to happen again and again?

If you've outlined the procedure in a handbook, volunteers can find the needed information anytime…without phoning you at 10:30 on a Saturday night. A well-written, clear handbook intercepts and answers many questions before they reach you.

3. Orientation handbooks are empowering.

Giving volunteers information in written form empowers them to make many decisions without having to ask for information. They'll know the church's philosophy of discipline and how they'll be reviewed.

4. Orientation handbooks require you to set policies.

Orientation handbooks force you—and other ministry leaders—to think through policies and procedures that affect volunteers. What should volunteers do if a tornado warning sounds while they're working with children at church? What are appropriate boundaries to respect in the adult–teenager mentoring program? How will volunteers be evaluated?

You can't write policies until you've made hard decisions about how situations should generally be handled, and that often takes some discussion among church leaders. But that's a good thing: The time and energy you invest in creating policies is time and energy volunteers don't have to exert wondering what to do when situations arise.

5. Orientation handbooks establish expectations.

If you expect volunteers to uphold standards, you've got to make clear what those standards are. If you don't want to see gossip, have a policy on confidentiality established. If you expect all volunteers to attend worship services regularly, say so.

And a word about standards: If you expect something of paid staff, expect it from unpaid staff, too. It's a double standard to insist that no paid staff smoke on church property but then put out ashtrays for the unpaid staff. Hold everyone to the same high standards. Doing less will confuse church members who don't see all that much difference between the associate pastor of Christian education (a paid staff position) and the Sunday school superintendent (an unpaid staff position).

> "If you expect something of paid staff, expect it from unpaid staff, too."

Besides, when you expect less of unpaid staff than paid staff, you demean your volunteers. Treat them like professionals, too.

So you need a volunteer handbook. Does that mean you have to have it ready for that initial formal orientation meeting? And do you really have to sit there and read it out loud?

The fact is that reading a long list of policies to volunteers accomplishes little. Volunteers won't remember what you said, and the policies won't impact their behavior. It's largely a waste of time if you're trying to teach volunteers information.

> ## Everyone knows this stuff counts.

But here's what it does accomplish (and even our friend Denise noticed it on her first day at the new job): *When you stop and read the handbook, it communicates how very important the material in the handbook is to the organization—and to the new volunteer or employee.* You draw attention to it. You shine a spotlight on it. And everyone knows that no matter what, this stuff counts.

Many companies and churches don't go to the lengths Denise's company did—they don't expect employees to read handbook policies aloud. Instead, they distribute handbooks and set a deadline by which employees must return a form stating the handbook has been read.

We'd like to suggest you adapt that procedure slightly. Distribute handbooks at your first formal orientation meeting. Also distribute a Volunteer Handbook Acknowledgement Form (p. 197) that volunteers must sign and return before they're allowed to serve in their volunteer role.

But what if you're a small church? Everyone knows everyone, and it's easy to explain to people how things work and what to do. Why bother with creating a handbook full of policies everyone already knows?

Even if you're in a church of 50 members, your volunteer ministry needs written policies in a handbook. Here's why...

- **Policies help resolve problems and eliminate hazards.**

A friend of ours is a lifeguard at a city pool. When he was hired, he thought his job would be to sit on a platform diligently watching the water, ever prepared to toss aside his whistle and clipboard and dive in to drag out a drowning swimmer.

His supervisor straightened the young man out.

"Your job first and foremost is not to rescue people who are victims of accidents or stupidity," the supervisor said. "Your first job is to keep people from having accidents or doing anything stupid."

During the course of his summer, the young man never once dove in to save someone. But more times than he could count, he kept children from running on the slick cement around the pool and enforced rules that kept weak swimmers out of the deep water. The lifeguard discovered that the pool policies he'd at first thought were silly actually kept people safe.

Your volunteer ministry policies can accomplish the same thing: Keep volunteers from getting into deep water without realizing it.

> **Your volunteer ministry policies can keep volunteers from getting into deep water.**

It may seem like a perfectly logical thing for Jack Smith to drop off a couple kids from the youth group after the meeting, and since Alisa's house is near his, it just stands to reason Jack will take Alisa, a 17-year-old girl, home last.

So there Jack is in the car at night, alone with a high school junior. Not smart.

A written policy about never having an adult with a minor in a car alone could have prevented Jack from ever making this mistake by setting a boundary beyond which he couldn't go.

- **Policies clarify responsibilities.**

  Knowing who is responsible to make decisions when the roof leaks is a good thing for the Sunday school teacher who stops by the building on a Saturday afternoon to pick up curriculum and notices an inch of water in the church basement.

  If your volunteer handbook doesn't have a page titled "Who You Gonna Call?" add one—fast. But do it by the title of the person responsible, not the name. When the Sunday school teacher sees she should call the "building and grounds deacon," she can then check the phone list to see who that is. Remember, keeping the phone list and the handbook separate saves you from having to constantly update the handbook when people fill new roles or phone numbers change.

- **Policies provide stability and continuity.**

  Over the course of a few years, you may have a complete turnover in volunteer staff in some area of ministry. You'll still be able to deliver a consistent level of service if everyone is on the same page concerning expectations—and the policies in your volunteer handbook can deliver those expectations.

- **Handbooks will help you provide a thorough orientation.**

  Encourage volunteers to highlight items as they read through their handbooks. Then at your next team meeting, discuss the policies—answering questions and highlighting the policies that you think are most important.

  You'll be able to move through the material more quickly if everyone has read the handbook, and you'll know if something in the handbook is unclear because those are the sections that will generate the most questions.

  Be sure volunteers write their names in their handbooks, too. Be clear that every volunteer is to have a copy of the handbook, to read it, and to affirm that he or she has read the entire document.

And make sure you keep track of who's read the handbook. You'll need that information when it's time to update or add a policy and issue a new handbook or replace selected pages in handbooks.

Also, your insurance company may offer discounts on liability coverage if you can demonstrate that no volunteer is placed until after having read policies about issues like child safety, sexual harassment, and confidentiality. Check with your insurance provider to see if any such discount is available to you.

When volunteers turn in their Volunteer Handbook Acknowledgment Form, keep the signed forms in their files. This documentation may be helpful should your church ever face civil litigation.

Feel free to adapt the Volunteer Handbook Acknowledgment Form to fit your unique situation. It's merely a template; have it reviewed by your legal counsel, and make whatever changes are appropriate. Also, be mindful that a signed form may have no impact whatsoever in the case of litigation…but it is one way to prove you attempted to communicate important policies.

Still not convinced? Then think about this…

- **Policies make managing a program easier.**

   Because policies include the "what," often the "why," and occasionally the "how" of a decision, you don't have to rethink situations each time they arise. Some of that has already been done and formalized; you can simply determine if circumstances warrant making an exception.

   Look—every volunteer ministry makes policy decisions frequently. They just don't call them "policy decisions" or write them down. It may be that your developing policies is as easy as reviewing the decisions your leadership has made lately and getting those decisions down on paper. One example of how that might look is on page 205. It's a list of policies related to the nursery at First Christian Church—see how many decisions have been captured in simple policy statements.

   Be proactive, too. Lots of policies are developed because something has gone wrong and nobody wants it to

> " Be proactive, too. "

happen again. So do this: Think about what might reasonably be expected to go wrong, and decide how you'll handle it now—before the bus breaks down, the power goes out, or the hurricane hits. Put your plan in writing.

Your handbook of policies won't be an imposition on your volunteers. In fact, your volunteers will welcome having the clarity and reassurance of the handbook.

Types of Policies

A word about policies before you begin writing them for your handbook: Policies are not all created equal. Some are non-negotiable, and others are very negotiable. Let's take a look at both categories.

1. Identify non-negotiable policies.

Some policies reflect local or federal laws. That you're working with volunteers rather than paid staff or operating in a church rather than a company doesn't change the law. It's real—and you need to always be meeting or exceeding the requirements of the law.

> You need to always be meeting or exceeding the requirements of the law.

In Romans 13 we read:

> *Everyone must submit himself to the governing authorities, for there is no authority except that which God has established. The authorities that exist have been established by God. Consequently, he who rebels against the authority is rebelling against what God has instituted, and those who do so will bring judgment on themselves.* (Romans 13:1-2)

If local building codes require you to have no more than 120 people in a room, don't let the 121st person through the door. If the Health Department insists you maintain your church kitchen at a certain level of cleanliness because you serve meals to the homeless twice per week, amaze the health inspector with how the floor sparkles and the food preparation meets every requirement.

And if federal law says you shouldn't sexually harass someone, don't do it. Ever. Period.

In some cases churches are able to bypass or be exempted from statutes that apply elsewhere—but why would you want to not measure up? If civil policies are about respecting the rights and dignity of people, be very, very careful about deciding they don't apply to you.

When you create your handbook and review it with volunteers, be clear that non-negotiable policies are just that: non-negotiable. Breaking them will result in being separated from volunteer opportunities in the church, at minimum, and in some cases, civil prosecution.

2. Consider negotiable policies.

Some policies are simply principles you've put in place to guide action. They're not laws. They can be bent or broken without dramatic consequences.

For instance, if your policy is to have Sunday school teachers sign on for six-month terms of service, that's a decision you've already made. You might have created that policy to help ensure consistency for the children in the Sunday school.

But if a woman who's taught Sunday school for just four months were to suddenly lose her husband, you wouldn't try to force her to complete her term of service. You could easily make an exception—and probably should make an exception.

The point: These policies are set in wet cement. Exceptions can be made, but be judicious about how often and for what reasons you make exceptions. In general, make exceptions rarely and only for good cause. A policy that's not applied fairly and consistently will quickly become a point of conflict.

Here are categories of negotiable policies you'll want to include in your handbook.

How-to-get-things-done policies—These policies concern themselves with how tasks are completed. For example, the volunteer serving as the church secretary will undoubtedly get phone calls—and those calls need to be handled professionally. One policy you might put in place for your entire volunteer ministry is that every phone call, e-mail, or other message must be responded to within 24 hours.

If the volunteer serving in the church office happens to miss the mark and returns a call two days late, will the volunteer be fired? No—but it will be cause for a discussion and review of the position expectation so the volunteer understands the importance of the policy.

When-to-get-things-done policies—If your volunteers are reimbursed for expenses, someone in the accounting office wants those expense reports on time so he or she can close out the month.

Don't expect volunteers to have the same sense of urgency about your deadlines that you have—unless you tell them those deadlines are important.

What-to-do-and-not-do policies—These policies explain what volunteers can and cannot do. They set boundaries that help define what appropriate relationships look like.

These policies may be negotiable or non-negotiable; it depends on what boundary will be crossed.

A negotiable policy may involve whether a Sunday school teacher can buy a child a birthday present. The answer: Certainly—but only if it's small, and only if it's something the teacher does for every child in his class.

These policies may also identify a boundary that a volunteer cannot cross, such as "borrowing" offering money as a short-term loan or inviting a student to go on a date. Crossing that sort of boundary elevates the issue to a non-negotiable policy.

What Should—and Shouldn't—Be in Your Volunteer Orientation Handbook

First, here's what *shouldn't* be there…

- Don't include organizational charts with names attached, phone lists, or anything else that's likely to need frequent updating. Ideally, you'll make changes in the handbook infrequently and only when there's an addition or change in policies.

- Don't include anything that you don't intend to enforce. Companies have found that if they're lax about enforcing one part of an employee handbook (drug testing, for instance) then employees can be justified in assuming that other policies (taking unannounced vacations, for example) won't be enforced, either. You won't find yourself in court trying to fire volunteers because they didn't give two weeks' notice before heading off to Montana to go elk hunting, but the principle has merit. If you aren't going to take something in your handbook seriously, don't include it.

- Don't include the little stuff. If your pet peeve is when nursery workers forget to empty the diaper pail on Sundays, the place to deal with that is in a training session with nursery workers. Don't add a separate section in the handbook about WHAT TO DO WITH STINKY STUFF. Use your handbook to focus on the larger, more general issues.

- Anything vague or cute should be cut from your handbook. Humor is fine, and if it's part of your culture and you encourage it, you'll want to let it shine through. But don't let humor or cuteness interfere with the

> "Anything vague or cute should be cut."

clarity of your handbook. Write to ensure you're not misunderstood. Use crisp, definite language. Say what you mean.

- Any specifics that are covered in position descriptions. Keep things simple: Let position descriptions speak for themselves.

That's what *shouldn't* clutter up a handbook. But what should be in a handbook? And how do you keep your handbook from becoming a 300-page manual that few can lift and no one will read?

You'll greatly increase the value of your handbook if you use it to communicate the information that doesn't change—and you communicate the information briefly.

That is, you don't need to deliver the last word on who brings the donuts on Sunday mornings, and how you really should bring a variety that includes cream-filled, nut-covered, glazed, and also plain donuts; that a box of glazed donuts might be easy but will fail to please some of the teachers—and you can probably guess which ones they are, isn't it obvious?—and, by the way, don't forget the cinnamon twists—they're the director's favorites. Just say snacks are available in the teachers' prep room on Sundays.

Be brief. Be clear.

Handbook Policy Essentials

Here are eleven areas you should address in your policy handbook. They're in no particular order; they're all important.

- **Your ministry's mission, vision, and values**

  Include the mission statement, vision statement, and a brief description of what you value. Be sure what you include is consistent with your overall church's values, mission, and vision.

  If your ministry places a special emphasis on teamwork, communication, diversity, quality, or another value, briefly define that value and describe what it looks like in your setting.

- **The general organizational structure of your ministry**

  Without naming names, describe who reports to whom. This is your chance to proactively reroute most phone calls away from yourself, so be thorough!

  Provide the organizational chart here; the easily updated phone list you hand out with the handbook will supply the details. You did remember to identify each person on your phone list by ministry role, too, didn't you? If not, add that information. It doesn't help if in the handbook you instruct teachers to call their section supervisors as identified on the phone list and then the phone list doesn't say who does what.

- **Dress codes and other behavior standards**

  If staff members aren't to use tobacco or alcohol while serving a term as a volunteer, say so. If that prohibition extends only to the times volunteers are actually serving, say that instead. Be clear where you can be, especially on behaviors that are black and white, done or not done.

  > Be clear where you can be.

  Some of those standards may be abundantly clear, such as...

  - No pierced body parts visible (other than simple earrings),

  - No smoking on campus, and

  - No fad clothing (for example, grunge or gothic).

  It's trickier when the behaviors involve interpretation, such as what constitutes "modest" apparel. Imprecise terms such as "modestly" and "professionally" leave a lot of gray area. How high can a skirt go and still be modest? How tight can jeans be and still be professional? Is it even professional to wear jeans? Who decides if someone has violated the policy, and who's going to tell the offender? How should it be resolved?

  Your policy isn't the place to nit-pick about the number of inches a hemline can rise above the knee or precisely what a T-shirt slogan can or can't say. Your goal isn't to create a comprehensive rulebook, but to briefly communicate standards.

  Most volunteers are ready and eager to cheerfully comply with standards— once the standards are clear. So if you use vague words, supply a couple of examples of what you mean. Volunteers will get the message.

  And here's a tip: Should someone show up to teach in clothing that's inappropriate, ask a leader of the same sex to take the offender aside and calmly suggest that the individual change clothes and then return to the volunteer role. Be careful not to communicate condemnation or spiritual superiority, but instead a gentle, caring redirection to what "modest" means in the context of the volunteer setting.

- **Equipment and facility usage**

  Is it okay to use the church's copier to make a copy of your son's social studies report? Is it okay to use the computer in the accounting office to look up possible condo rentals in Vail for next winter? to look up stock prices? to look up porn sites? What exactly are your policies regarding the use of the church's equipment and facilities? Your handbook is a great place to explain them.

- **The performance evaluation system**

  When and how do you evaluate volunteers? Describe the process so there are no surprises later. Having this spelled out is reassuring to volunteers because it communicates you care enough to actually come and see what they're doing and to help them improve. A performance evaluation system says you value them and their work.

- **Safety information**

  Include evacuation plans, severe storm plans, the location of first aid kits, and a notification system to use in case someone is hurt. Be especially brief here; when there's blood on the floor, the average person will remember just one or two things, not a complex maze of instructions.

  And don't forget to include standards about the situations in which adults can be with teenagers or children. What seems harmless at the time can take on sinister tones when viewed under the harsh light of a police inquiry or the direct questions of parents. Your policies can keep volunteers from getting themselves into trouble.

- **Security information**

  Do children need to be checked in and out? What's your system for that? Must outside doors be secured in some areas? Who has permission to activate or deactivate an alarm system? Spell out—briefly and clearly—what principles and standards you're maintaining in the effort to keep people secure.

Include a statement about which positions require background checks, and never, ever fail to enforce this policy. List what other screening, training, and supervision your church provides, too. And include a church policy statement on confidentiality and privacy.

- **Logistics**

Are volunteers to park in a certain spot so visitors can have the closest parking spots? Is there a specific system for reserving audio-visual equipment or getting a broken chair repaired? Where are mops and buckets kept? A brief review of this information will help volunteers fit into the church's procedures.

- **Grievance procedures**

Not everything will go smoothly 100 percent of the time. When a volunteer feels he or she has a legitimate complaint against a supervisor, what should the volunteer do?

> **Not everything will go smoothly 100 percent of the time.**

Jesus provides some excellent guidelines for conflict resolution in the book of Matthew. Consider…

But I tell you that anyone who is angry with his brother will be subject to judgment. Again, anyone who says to his brother, "Raca," is answerable to the Sanhedrin. But anyone who says, "You fool!" will be in danger of the fire of hell. Therefore, if you are offering your gift at the altar and there remember that your brother has something against you, leave your gift there in front of the altar. First go and be reconciled to your brother; then come and offer your gift. (Matthew 5:22-23)

But I tell you: Love your enemies and pray for those who persecute you. (Matthew 5:44)

If your brother sins against you, go and show him his fault, just between the two of you. If he listens to you, you have won your brother over. But if he will not listen, take one or two others along, so that "every matter may be established by the testimony of two or three witnesses." If he refuses to listen to them, tell it to the church; and if he refuses to listen even to the church, treat him as you would a pagan or a tax collector. (Matthew 18:15-17)

> **In short: Forgive, confront, seek resolution.**

In short: Forgive, confront, seek resolution. It's a good idea to apply those principles to your situation if there's dissent in the ranks. If your policy about conflict specifies that volunteers should talk first to someone who can actually do something to resolve the situation, you'll eliminate a great deal of gossip.

• Career development opportunities

Volunteers have careers, too. Some volunteers have several of them—one inside the church and one outside the walls of your building.

Take Eddie for instance. On Sunday morning he's an adult class leader, taking a group of parents through a study of good parenting habits. But on Monday morning, he's a medical doctor, explaining to patients why they should exercise.

Eddie has two careers—one as a teacher and one as a doctor—and he wants to grow in both of them.

What opportunities can you offer Eddie that will help him grow? A master teacher mentor who will assess his teaching and facilitating skills? That will help Eddie in both of his careers, so you'll find him eager to sign on.

If you can offer mentoring or training courses, a library of useful training materials, or any other development opportunities, tell volunteers about them.

- **Scheduled events and activities**

  Do you have quarterly training meetings? an annual banquet? staff meetings on Sunday mornings? If you have regular programming, identify it, and be clear about whether attendance is encouraged, optional, or mandatory.

Informal Orientation Process

Don't think distributing a handbook of policies completes the orientation process. Handbooks are helpful—but they aren't the last word in orientation.

In addition to orienting new volunteers, be sure to let existing volunteers who will work alongside the new faces know that someone is coming. Make introductions, and encourage existing volunteers to connect with new people over a cup of coffee.

Informal orientation will happen only if volunteer peers are talking. True, you don't know what the veteran volunteers might say, but they'll say it anyway—you might as well encourage the process.

Also, see that the paid or unpaid staff members who will supervise the new volunteers quickly arrange individual meetings with their new reports. The relationship volunteers have with their supervisors will make or break the volunteers' experience. It's the supervisors who will shape the volunteers' work flow and are positioned to best provide training and encouragement.

Some churches have found it helpful to create a video that includes orientation material. If done well, this can be a benefit—but it shouldn't (and can't) replace person-to-person contact.

Finally, arrange for a follow-up program in three to six months. Get the same group of volunteers back together for a "reunion," and see how they're doing in their roles. If you're in a large church, it's possible they haven't talked since their formal orientation program. They'll

> **Arrange for a follow-up program in three to six months.**

enjoy seeing each other again and swapping stories, and you'll have the chance to administer the same test you gave them after the first orientation program.

Compare test scores and comments. You may find that something the new volunteers rated poorly on their first test is ranked highly on the second test. Use what you learn to shape future orientation programs and processes.

And here's a challenge for you to consider taking: When you've completed your orientation process, give each volunteer a copy of the Volunteer Bill of Rights you'll find on page 207. It summarizes the basic expectations volunteers should see met. Are you delivering them? Some have to do with orientation and training, some with the design of your volunteer ministry.

Transition to Training

The formal orientation program covers the big-picture issues, but most of your volunteers' questions will be about their specific tasks. You probably aren't prepared to answer those questions; that's up to the volunteers' supervisors.

We'll focus on training next, and it's a piece of the puzzle that you'll find will challenge you like few other areas of volunteer leadership. Training requires you to set aside your preconceptions and do a great deal of listening well before you ever begin talking.

Training Volunteers

The benefits of providing training—for you, your church, and your volunteers.

We couldn't track down who said it first, but we spotted the saying on a bumper sticker: "If you think education is expensive, try ignorance."

It's true, isn't it? Education is expensive. Educating your volunteers through carefully designed training sessions is expensive—but consider what it costs if you let them operate in the dark.

What might happen if a nursery attendant doesn't understand the proper ways to provide security for babies?

What might happen if an elementary teacher doesn't know how to apply loving correction?

What might happen if a youth volunteer doesn't see anything wrong with letting the kids go unchaperoned at the youth lock-in?

What might happen if someone ushering thinks nobody will notice if he slips away from his post to grab a cup of coffee with friends over in the Hospitality Café?

What might happen if...?

Clearly ignorance is not bliss—not when it comes to working with volunteers.

Why Training Is Worth the Effort—and Cost

- **It's how you build in excellence.**

  When you embrace the idea of training, you get to decide how excellent your programming will be. If you don't do training, you take what you can get.

  Think about it: If you've placed appropriate people in volunteer roles, you know they're capable. There's at least a good chance they can accomplish the job set before them.

  And they're motivated—they signed up, went through interviewing and placement, and completed orientation. They want to deliver great service.

  But there's a lot they don't know, and in any volunteer role, what you don't know can hurt you—or at least hurt your performance. Your volunteers will stumble along doing their best, but it's completely possible for them to make the same mistake over and over again—because they don't know any better.

  If you want excellence, training is worth the effort.

- **It's how you make volunteers happy.**

  Training is also worth the effort if you're looking for happy volunteers.

  > "Training is worth the effort."

  Nobody likes feeling incompetent, especially when the responsibility is important. To you, a volunteer stuffing inserts into bulletins may not look like he's doing anything complicated, but you're wrong. He's given up a morning with his wife to be at the church, sitting in a corner of the office, sticking pieces of paper inside a bulletin cover. His back is acting up because he's sardined at a table that isn't really comfortable, but he's not complaining. He's praying for the people who will receive the bulletins on Sunday morning.

  He's not doing grunt work. He's doing ministry.

So imagine how happy he'll be if, as he wraps up the 500th bulletin cover, you point out that the yellow insert should have gone in before the brown one.

Want happy volunteers? Training is worth the effort.

- **It's how you hold down costs.**

  True, training volunteers can be expensive in terms of preparation time and photocopies. But imagine what it would cost if you had to hire professionals to do everything volunteers do?

  People wiser than us have pointed out that if you want to do a job in the most cost-effective way, you need to clearly understand what you're trying to accomplish before you get started and decide how you'll proceed. That's true with building highways, and it's true with trimming the church lawn.

  Don't let people learn from trial and error. You'll pay for each error.

  Want to hold down costs? Training is worth the effort.

- **It's how you respect the calling of volunteers.**

  If you truly believe that God brings volunteers into ministry roles so they can grow closer to him and use their spiritual gifts, abilities, skills, and passions, your job is to equip them. You'll want to encourage and coach them. And that means providing training opportunities so they get ever more capable in service.

  Want to cooperate with God's purposes? Training is worth the effort.

  There's no reason to fail to provide training, just excuses.

  If you're directing volunteers in your church, you'll find yourself in the role of "trainer." You may be training volunteers who report directly to you or training other ministry leaders how to train the volunteers who report to them. However your church ministries are configured, training will play a significant role in them.

  Let's consider your role of trainer.

The Role of Trainers

If your mental image of a trainer is someone who's standing in front of a room, holding a clipboard and speaking to rows of attentive learners, you've got some challenges ahead of you.

That view of training—the expert who is lecturing students—is both out of date and ultimately ineffective.

Here's the thing: There are talented people who make careers out of becoming ever more expert trainers. They study how people learn, and how to set up environments where adults are best able to focus and retain knowledge. They study learning styles, presentation styles, and what tools can bridge the two. Every day they study what works, what doesn't work, and what could work better.

And to think: Training is just one of the hats you have to wear!

> **Don't worry—you're up to the challenge.**

Don't worry—you're up to the challenge. Training, at heart, is teaching—and if you're like most volunteer ministry leaders, you've had considerable experience helping others learn new information and build new skills.

Effective training really breaks down to five key responsibilities, each of which you can handle, and most or all of which you've already mastered.

See for yourself.

1. Prepare and prepare some more.

The first place you'll do preparation is the training material itself.

We'll dig into how to develop appropriate content for training sessions later in this volume, but for now, realize that effective training takes considerable effort and focus. It's not something you throw together at the last minute.

Plus, you need to prepare the volunteers themselves. In the sessions you lead, you'll put them at ease and share why the training they'll experience is important. As a trainer, it's your job to capture the volunteers' attention; don't assume they'll just give it to you. It's your job to create (and maintain) a compelling learning environment.

2. Explain the skill or task you're addressing in training.

Let's say you're showing office volunteers how to operate the photocopy machine. The volunteers are responsible for creating, designing, and copying flyers for an upcoming event. Operating "Ol' Jambox" (as your antiquated machine is affectionately known) is a skill they'll need.

The trick is for you to break down the information into manageable bites and build on information the volunteers already have.

3. Show as well as tell.

It's one thing to hear about how to do a task and another to see it demonstrated. Help volunteers grasp how to operate the office photocopy machine by actually pulling open drawers and pushing buttons. Show volunteers where the paper goes in, where it comes out, and how to find the fire extinguisher if Ol' Jambox decides to burst into flames—again.

4. Involve volunteers in actually doing the task or skill.

Volunteers' confidence grows when they have the opportunity to perform the tasks or practice using the skill while you're there to coach them through it. A trainer learns to monitor closely at first, then gradually step back as volunteers develop competence and good habits. You'll help volunteers process their newfound information as they work with the copier.

5. Review and retrain.

As volunteers operate Ol' Jambox, give them encouragement and honest feedback. Maybe one of the volunteers seems to have a feel for communicating with the quirky copier and is able to coax a ream of forms out of the machine before papers start to jam. Perhaps another volunteer needs to quit stabbing the buttons, hoping to intimidate the machine into working at all.

Review what volunteers have learned, and provide the tweaking—retraining—that's required to get everyone up to speed.

That's it: a trainer's job in a nutshell.

> Trainers are teachers.

Trainers are teachers—teachers who work with adults, and who facilitate learning by using hands-on, active learning. That's a win for everyone, because skills and information are more easily learned and retained by volunteers when experienced in a practical, active way.

Plus, it's way more fun to teach!

As we consider how to design a training session, see how interaction and involvement are woven into the process. They're there for a reason.

How to Design Training Sessions That Work

Nine strategic steps that let you deliver on-target training sessions—every time.

An effective training session starts long before volunteers walk into the room, fill out their name tags, and mingle by the coffeepot. The actual session is the part of the process people associate with training, but it's only the tip of the iceberg.

If you experience a training session that's informative, effective, and useful, you can bet the trainer began preparing for the session weeks before.

That's the decision you have to make first: Will you be disciplined in preparing for training sessions? If not, seek out someone who will, and delegate the training function of your ministry to that person. Training is too important to hope that when you wing it, something good will come out of the experience.

Training requires thoughtful preparation. There's no shortcut.

Assuming you believe that training is worthy of your best effort, go through the following nine-step process to create on-target sessions that accomplish your goals.

> "Training requires thoughtful preparation."

Step 1: Determining the Need

What do people want and need to know?

Some experts call it "gap analysis": identifying the space between the existing experience and knowledge of your volunteers, and what experience and knowledge they'll need to accomplish a task.

It's that gap between what they've got and what they'll need that training seeks to fill—so you'd better do a good job identifying the gap. Providing training for the wrong experiences and knowledge is useless.

Consider the experiences of a friend of ours named Brian...

Brian was determined to make his school basketball team after failing to make the squad the previous year. "I was the last guy cut," Brian remembers. "It about crushed me."

So Brian attended basketball camps and spent afternoons at city courts ,where he sharpened his skills in game after game of pick-up ball.

"I'd always been a timid player," Brian says, "afraid to get under the hoop and mix it up. But if you're not willing to throw a few elbows, you got eaten alive out on the public courts—especially the ones where the really good street players hung out. Nobody called fouls out there; it was a matter of pride. You either intimidated the other players or you died."

> ## "Brian watched— and learned."

Brian watched—and learned. He mimicked better players and learned how to shave half-steps while driving to the basket. He practiced moves that eventually had him winning instead of watching, taking high-fives from players he respected.

Brian went from timid to intimidating. "I learned to take it to the bucket," he says. "Get in my way and you were going down. I could usually get around you, over you, under you—something. But if I couldn't—well, I went through you."

So Brian felt strong when he tried out for the varsity team his junior year.

"I put on a show for them right off the start," he says. "Once I had the ball, I angled and cut my way to the basket. Every time. I smoked the defense during our first scrimmage. Scored 28 points."

Brian went home sure he had impressed the coaches. And he had—they cut him from the tryouts the next day.

Stunned, Brian asked the head coach what had happened. He pointed out that he wasn't the player he'd once been, timid and shy. Now he was a scorer—and he'd proved it.

That's when the coach gave Brian the news: Brian hadn't been cut from the squad the previous year because he lacked the ability to score or because he'd been weak on hitting the boards and bringing down rebounds; he'd been cut because the coach didn't think he was a team player.

And if anything, Brian was even worse now. He didn't pass, he didn't run plays, he just hot-dogged the ball and left the rest of the team standing around.

Brian had trained hard to improve—but in the wrong skill.

"I never made the team until my senior year," Brian says. "But I was high man on assists that year."

Ouch. Brian had done a poor job with "gap analysis."

Do your needs analysis carefully. Fixing the wrong thing doesn't move volunteers ahead; it leaves them further behind.

And it's important you not confuse activity with accomplishment when it comes to training. Holding training sessions is only useful if there are appropriate outcomes (ones that help fill the gap) that can be demonstrated by the volunteers. Do they know how to operate the photocopy machine after your training session? That's actually easy to determine: Have them show you how to do it.

Did they truly learn? Also easy: Call them back in a week and ask them to demonstrate their retained skills.

Volunteers themselves may help you with needs analysis. Ask volunteers to tell you what they need to know. Ask their supervisors what they need to know. You may get a glimmer of what's needed when you interview or survey the people served by your volunteers.

> **Ask volunteers what they need to know.**

If Jack thinks he's doing a great job delivering Christian education and his leader agrees, but children aren't learning anything, there's a gap—and a need for training!

When thinking about training, start by determining what the volunteers need to be doing differently as a result of the training. Is the need they're experiencing one that can be met through more information? through using a new skill? through a shift in attitude?

How you understand the need sets the course of the entire training session.

Step 2: Establishing Objectives

Okay, let's be realistic: A one- or two-hour training session isn't going to completely revolutionize how Jack teaches in the fourth-grade class. One session isn't going to somehow toggle Jack's effectiveness switch on so kids start learning, especially if you're going to present the training to the entire Sunday school teaching staff and can't focus solely on Jack.

But you can do this: Write clear objectives you think you can achieve, given the number of learners, the various settings in which they deliver Christian education, and the amount of time you have for the session.

Narrow down what you're trying to accomplish. Instead of "figure out how to have every teacher become effective in engaging children and doubling students' learning" (lofty, but not probable), zero in on one skill classroom teachers could use to improve their teaching. Classroom management techniques, perhaps, or skills related to using active-learning techniques.

> Narrow down what you're trying to accomplish.

Write behavioral objectives—what volunteers will be able to do at the end of the training session. It may have to be demonstrated through role plays (as in the case of Jack dealing with his students), but be certain that volunteers can do a show and tell with the new skill or information.

And be absolutely certain that possessing the new skill or information will help address the need you identified in step 1.

Step 3: Creating the Evaluation Tool

Decide how you'll have volunteers prove they've "gotten it" at the end of the training session, and create that evaluation tool now. Be specific, and design it so it answers the question "How will volunteers prove they've achieved the session's objectives?"

Seems backward, doesn't it? Why create the test before you've created the training session?

It's because the evaluation tool pinpoints your destination. It identifies where you want to end up at the end of the session when volunteers are walking out the door. It measures the outcomes you identified in step 2.

Step 4: Brainstorming the Training Session

Working alone or with colleagues, think about the evaluation tool you've identified. Write it out, and tape it to the far end of a white board. Then, with a marker in hand, ask, "Given where the learners are now, what do they need to learn to let them pass this evaluation exercise?"

The answer to your question—the steps and skills—are the content of the training session. You've created your session outline.

Step 5: Writing a Training Session

Arrange your outline in a logical order. Before you flesh it out, though, ask yourself the following questions. Your answers will help you shape *how* you deliver the content of the training session to your volunteers.

> Arrange your outline in a logical order.

And be warned: This will take some time. You're pausing to consider how to tailor the training session so it powerfully connects with your volunteers—all your volunteers.

Think of it this way: Pretty much anyone can wander onto a softball diamond. Anyone can walk to the pitcher's mound. Anyone can stand there, face the catcher crouching behind home plate, and throw a softball to the catcher. It's only 46 feet, so it's not terribly difficult.

You lob the ball, and it gets to the catcher—either in the air, on the bounce, or rolling along in the dirt. If you lower the definition of "pitching" far enough, anyone can do it.

But to sizzle that ball into the strike zone, blistering it into the catcher's mitt—that takes some effort. It requires practice and preparation. And it's the sort of pitch that gets fans up on their feet and cheering.

Don't just settle for lobbing training sessions at your volunteers; do what's necessary to make each one spectacular, streaking straight across home plate. It comes down to delivery—and your answers to these questions will help you find and hit the strike zone every time.

- **How will I present this session in such a way that volunteers care?**

Without motivation, there's no lasting learning—so always establish to a volunteer's satisfaction why a skill must be mastered or information learned. What problem of the volunteer's will it solve so the volunteer will enthusiastically embrace the work required to accomplish the outcomes set for this training?

> "Without motivation, there's no lasting learning."

- **How can I build on information volunteers already possess?**

Do you actually know what people already know? You can establish this by using a pretest at the beginning of the training session and then adjusting the session depending on what you discover.

Clearly, this is a risky maneuver. You may discover that half of your volunteers could lead the session, and the other half have no clue about the topic. More likely you'll find that volunteers fall along a continuum stretching from incompetent to very competent.

For instance, our Sunday school teacher friend, Jack, probably already knows something about classroom discipline. What he knows may be wrong, or it may be right, but he knows something.

If you're a beginning trainer, you may wish to skip pretests for a few sessions until your confidence builds. But then by all means use them—they'll let you know precisely how to meet the needs of your specific audience.

And if you're lucky, you may find you have a valuable resource in the room that you can tap to make the training session even stronger.

> "If you're lucky you may find you have a valuable resource in the room."

If you find yourself in a situation where someone in your audience is truly better informed than you and is intent on letting everyone know it, defuse the situation by reminding your audience that everyone will have time to speak later in the session. Most people take the hint.

- **How can I address various learning styles during the training?**

  There have been several attempts to categorize learning styles, and each of them agrees on this point: Talking *at* people isn't the way to go.

  There are people who learn best by seeing a demonstration and those who learn best by diving in and trying things themselves. There are logical thinkers and people who learn best when they're interacting with others. Still other people learn best through introspection…or through music…or through experiencing nature.

  How can you possibly present all of the information in each of those styles?

  You can't…but you can make sure there's something for everyone during the training session.

> "Make sure there's something for everyone during the training session."

For example, if you're helping Sunday school teachers learn how to handle classroom discipline, include a few of these elements...

- Have volunteers tell stories about situations that have arisen. This will snag your verbal and linguistic learners.

- Ask visual learners to design a classroom setting that would minimize disruptions. Where would the teacher be? the students? What furniture would or wouldn't be in the room?

- Ask musically inclined people to suggest a theme song for the chaotic classroom. What popular song (or classic song) sums up what it's like?

- Recruit kinesthetic learners to act out a skit about a typical classroom discipline challenge.

- Suggest that logical learners brainstorm ideas about what Sunday school teachers can do to overcome the discipline challenges.

- Issue this challenge to the naturalists in your audience: What lessons are there in nature about how to deal with disruptions from children? (And no, teachers can't eat their young!)

- Give interpersonal learners the chance to work together to plan an event where people could find answers around the challenge of classroom discipline. Who would attend? What would happen?

- For intrapersonal learners, ask them to describe how they feel when children sabotage their lessons.

Will all these fit in a single training session? Probably not. It will help if you have a breakout session that allows people to choose between several of the activities so they can plug in where they're most comfortable. And even if you can't accommodate every learning style, the more you can use, the more people in your audience will think you're speaking directly to them.

- **How can I make this session interactive?**

It's less difficult than you might imagine. Including peer-to-peer discussion in small groups or pair-shares is a great place to start.

Consider breaking out small groups to each tackle a piece of a carefully identified problem, with each group then coming back with its piece of the jigsaw puzzle. This is a great way not only to be interactive but to build ownership of the solution that eventually emerges.

Look for places to effectively use activities, exercises, discussions of case studies, team building or teamwork, brainstorming—they're all ways to include interactive learning.

Picture the person who'll attend who's most likely to be thinking of something else. Maybe it's Jerry, who always appears to be taking notes but you know he is actually filling out work-related expense reports. Or Samantha, who drums her fingers and fidgets if she's forced to sit still for more than 10 minutes.

Here's your goal: Design a training session that Samantha can tolerate and that will have Jerry checking his watch when the session ends, wondering where the time went.

- **How can I intentionally encourage volunteers in the context of this training session?**

What will you say or do that affirms volunteers in their service and faithfulness? Saying "thanks for coming" is a good start, but you'll have more opportunity as the training session unfolds. Add to this list…

- Know the names of volunteers when they arrive. Greet them by name—before they fill out name tags.

- Know what each volunteer does in ministry so you can ask specific questions and keep the training relevant.

- Affirm individuals for their contributions.

- Pray for individuals, asking God to bless them.

"Affirm individuals for their contributions."

Once volunteers are serving in a ministry role, occasional training sessions may be the only face-to-face time you have with some volunteers. Don't miss the chance to remind them that what they do is ministry, and that their ministry is appreciated.

- **How can I encourage volunteers to grow in their relationship with Jesus in the context of this training session?**

Remember one of the core values of volunteer leadership: One outcome of participating as a volunteer needs to be growth in the volunteer's relationship with Jesus.

Never lose sight of this value! Let it slip from view and you're simply recruiting people to do jobs. You're no longer involving them in significant ministry that changes lives—including the volunteer's own life.

Ways you can encourage relational growth with Jesus at a training session include...

- Praying with the volunteers.

- Asking volunteers what impact their volunteer experience is having on their relationship with Jesus. Let them tell you!

- Sharing a devotion together, perhaps one prepared by one of the volunteers.

What else could you do? With your content outline and your answers to the questions listed above, you're ready to finish creating the training session. Keep in mind the limitations you face regarding time and space (no sense planning to illustrate teamwork by playing a full-court volleyball game if you'll meet in a classroom), and go to it. Craft a workshop that covers the material and integrates the insights you gained by thinking about how you'll shape the delivery of your training session.

Step 6: Developing a Great Opening

How you launch into your training session is very important. It's when you reel in your volunteers and get them focused and concentrating, or it's the precise moment you lose them—maybe for the entire session.

Because of that, be very intentional about how you begin your session.

> Be wary of humor.

A word of caution: Be wary of humor. If your joke falls flat, or your humor somehow offends a volunteer, you're sunk.

A stronger opening will be some way to illustrate the point that the subject matter you'll cover together will solve a problem experienced in the volunteers' lives. Establish that the training is relevant and there's a benefit, and you're home free.

Step 7: Deciding on an Icebreaker

Even if you suspect all your volunteers know each other, icebreakers are a good idea at the beginning of your session. Why? Because they do three important things:

- They focus attention. Your volunteers are tired, busy, and at least partially wishing they could be doing other things. When you get them actively involved, you force volunteers to be present in the moment.

- They're fun. Ask most volunteers what they expect to experience at a training session and you'll wait a long time before you hear "fun." That's because the expectation is that training is boring. Not true! Start your session out on the right foot by exceeding volunteers' expectations immediately with a few minutes of good, clean fun!

- And if the volunteers truly hate icebreakers, you unite them against a common enemy: you! Perhaps this is a bit overstated, but if you're enthusiastically asking volunteers to do something that stretches them past their comfort level, they'll all be on the same page. You can build from there by acknowledging their willingness to try new things and promising you'll never again ask each person to sing a verse of his or her favorite show tune.

Four Fool-Proof, Easy-Prep, No-Fail Icebreakers

Find the Fib

Ask each volunteer to tell three things about his or her life that nobody at the meeting knows—except one of the stories is a fib. This is easier for new people whose history is largely unknown, but everyone has something from their childhood that isn't generally known. A first job, an unusual skill, an odd experience while on vacation—they're all grist for the mill.

Have volunteers form groups of three or four and take turns sharing stories. Then after a volunteer talks, ask the other group members to vote on which story was a fib. Following the vote, let the storyteller reveal the truth.

Guess the Pet

This is a simple icebreaker that uses name tags. In addition to writing his or her name, ask each volunteer to also write the name of a childhood pet. After all the volunteers have arrived, form volunteers into groups of four, and try to guess what sort of animal the pet was, based on the name.

This icebreaker once rewarded the person who had a pet boa constrictor named "Fluffy"!

Decipher the Code

Another name tag icebreaker. In addition to writing his or her name, ask each volunteer to also write a number that has significance in his or her life.

For instance, if a woman was married on May 23, 1987, the number written would be 52387. If a man's childhood home was 1011 Pennway Lane, the number might be 1011. After all the volunteers have arrived, form volunteers into groups of four and try to decipher what the numbers mean by asking questions that have yes or no answers.

Step 8: Practicing

Never let the time you stand up in front of a group of volunteers be the first time you've run completely through a training session. Practice walking through the session at least twice to test the timing of the activities and to be sure your notes are clear to you.

Some ministry leaders actually do the entire training session with peers to get their feedback.

Also, this is a good time to think about how you'll set up the location where you'll be doing the training session. Do you need audio or visual equipment? Will you need to be able to control the lighting? Do the chairs need to be set up in any particular configuration or removed altogether? Are there props for you to gather or people who will be working with you in presenting the material? snacks or notepads and pens to have available? name tags to fill out before volunteers arrive?

Logistics are part of the practice session. Be sure you know what you'll need, and have it ready to go before the eleventh hour. The eleventh hour is reserved for prayer and whatever crisis comes up to throw you off track.

Step 9: Asking for and Valuing Feedback

Build two feedback loops into your training sessions. The first is already in place: the ability or inability of the volunteers to do what was set as an objective. If your training was effective, it should have had an impact on their abilities to meet the objective.

But use another feedback loop, too: surveys from volunteers who have gone through the training session.

A sample training session evaluation begins on page 199. Adapt it to suit your situation, but please note that unless you include open-ended questions to prompt a candid evaluation, you won't learn much from surveys. If you train enough volunteers at a time to make it practical for volunteers to believe their responses can be anonymous, remove the opportunity for volunteers to report their names. If you have ten or fewer volunteers in a session, they probably doubt they can stay anonymous anyway, so ask for names.

Those nine steps will guide you through designing on-target training sessions, but there are still things you could profit from knowing. Among them are the two dozen tips for trainers we've gathered from top-notch trainers from around the country and included in the next chapter.

Read through the list with a highlighter in hand. Mark those nuggets that you know would improve your training sessions or your skills as a trainer.

How to Get Volunteers to Actually Show Up for Training Sessions

Frank was busy. Things came up for Sarah. Jeff was unexpectedly called out of town on a job-related trip. Terri was on vacation. Joni's kids got sick. The in-laws dropped by unannounced for a visit at Mike's house. Hannah forgot. Dirk's dog died.

Host training sessions long enough and you'll be convinced there's no such thing as a new excuse—until you hear one. And you will hear one. It's frustrating to prepare training sessions and have people who have agreed to come—and who need the training—not show up.

Here are six things you can do to prompt higher attendance...

- **Realize it's true: Sometimes things do come up.**

  Very few of us have perfect attendance for anything. Be graceful when volunteers encounter illnesses, broken water heaters, emergency dental visits, and other schedule-changing events.

- **Be sure training is an up-front expectation.**

  Outline what's expected in terms of training in the job description. Mention it at meetings. Talk about it in newsletters. And always connect training with the benefits that come from it.

- **Provide lots of advance notice.**

  Schedule your meetings well in advance, and if possible make them consistent. It's easier to clear a spot on the calendar if it's predictable, such as the last Sunday evening of each month.

- **Remove obstacles.**

  Provide child care. Include a meal if the session approaches meal time. Be as adaptable and accommodating as possible.

- **Consider alternate training methods.**

  You probably can't get all your volunteers to set aside a full day for training. It just doesn't happen any more. If attendance for training events is slipping, perhaps you stop asking "When should we meet?" and start asking, "How would you like to receive training?"

  Options include:

  Mentoring—which can be arranged at the convenience of the mentor and mentoree.

  On-line training—that lets volunteers log on at their convenience.

  Independent study opportunities—which could include video courses, workbooks, books to read and review, and audio tapes.

Bite-size training—such as e-mails that address just one teaching skill, a text message with one training tip, or five-minute meetings on Sunday mornings before a worship service or between services.

Observation/coaching—which involves a trainer watching a volunteer in action and then giving specific feedback to the volunteer.

If a volunteer opts for non-traditional training, it will increase the amount of work you—or someone on your task force or board—will have to do. But the result is better trained volunteers.

- **Ask volunteers to write one-year training plans.**

  Remember, including people in a process builds buy-in to the process. Let volunteers know what training is available, what level of training is appropriate for their role, and ask them what sessions they wish to take. Hold volunteers accountable with regular check-ins.

Two Dozen Tips for Trainers

Training is art as well as science. Here are things top-notch trainers have discovered to be true—you can put them to use in your own volunteer training sessions today!

Training is a bit like cooking: It involves both science and art.

When you're trying for the perfect lasagna, you've got to master the science first. The temperature of the oven, the acidity of the tomato sauce, the thickness of the noodles—that's the science. It's unforgiving and non-negotiable. Mess up how long you leave the pan in the oven and you've either got lasagna soup or lasagna jerky. Neither is anything close to the perfect lasagna.

> "Training is a bit like cooking: It involves both science and art."

But master the science and now you can express your art. Exactly how much cheese do you add? And what kinds of cheese? Ah—that's when you start to develop the secret of your own family recipe. And you delight people lucky enough to get a dinner invitation to your house.

We hounded some excellent volunteer training "cooks" to get their secrets for successful training sessions. Here are the tips they shared. Two dozen that you can serve up to make your perfect training session even better.

1. Never settle for lecturing.

Find ways to involve the senses, and wrap stories into your training. Emotional content also touches people in significant ways. You'll notice you can remember the joke the pastor shared as a sermon introduction far longer than you can remember the sermon itself. Take advantage of the power of story.

2. Learning is most successful when stress from environment, emotional factors, and external commitments are reduced.

This is one reason that what happens in the first 5 minutes of your training session is so vitally important. If you can focus volunteers, convincing them to set aside their concerns for the duration of your training session, you'll see more learning happen.

Here's a technique that you can use if all else fails: Open the door into the hallway outside your room, and invite all the concerns and worries being experienced by your volunteers to wait outside. Tell volunteers they can pick up their concerns after the training session is over—but for the duration, those concerns will be waiting in the hall.

3. Past experience should be part of the present learning.

Build on what people already know—how they already think and what they already understand—and you'll find people are quicker to accept what you say.

4. What you present first and last will be retained in a disproportionate degree.

It's the way we tend to listen to each other: What's said first and last counts most. So start strong and sum up at the end; those two portions of your training are your best chance to make an impression.

5. Success reinforces learning.

It's better to cover something limited and do it so volunteers experience success than to attempt to cover more and fail. Break skill training into bite-size pieces. Dumping a ton of information on volunteers just buries them.

6. Volunteers learn at different speeds.

Obvious, huh? So why do we think one training session will have every volunteer emerge from the meeting on the same page and ready to go?

One benefit of having mentors work with volunteers is that there's room for individual coaching.

7. Learning and unlearning are continuous; review and practice are critical.

The good news is that people are always learning. The bad news is that they're always forgetting, too. If you want volunteers to sustain learning and stay good at something, provide for practice and review opportunities.

All learning is not like riding a bicycle: You don't automatically remember. Come to think of it, riding a bike isn't like riding a bike, either. Adults who jump back on after 20 years of not riding may wobble a lot. The learning curve may be shortened, but there's still a learning curve.

8. There's more than one reason to provide training sessions.

Here are examples of reasons you might create training sessions:

To impart knowledge—how to fill out an attendance sheet.

To develop specific skills—how to share your faith story with a child.

To modify attitudes—motivating a tired team to keep on trying.

To help individuals select a task—helping the youth group decide between a short-term mission project in Haiti or a ski retreat in Vail

To enable volunteers to identify with the ministry—sharing your vision and mission.

To increase volunteers' self-confidence—encouraging, motivating, and helping them see the positive outcomes of their work.

To respond to volunteers' personal needs—giving over-busy volunteers a better understanding of time management or life balance.

To accord volunteers status—communicating that volunteers are worth keeping, and keeping current.

> "What's your purpose in having a training session?"

To offer them an opportunity to opt out—letting everyone see what's going to be required when a new set of expectations is coming.

What's your purpose in having a training session?

9. Create a culture where growing in skills and knowledge is valued.

If you expect volunteers to be proactive about finding their own ways to grow in their skills and abilities, you've got to be intentional about creating opportunities for that to happen. Many of your volunteers have access to training through their companies or through purchasing their own books and magazines.

10. Set an expectation that training is part of serving.

In each position description be clear that training sessions, workshops, and other growth opportunities are part of the role. Ask for attendance at formal sessions you conduct, but suggest that volunteers find other avenues to grow, too.

11. Model behavior you want to see in volunteers.

What courses or workshops are *you* taking? books you're reading? mentoring you're experiencing? Talk about it enthusiastically when you're with volunteers.

12. Make training dollars available.

Okay, you can't afford to send everyone to a conference or the Equipping Institute this year. Can you afford to get subscriptions to appropriate magazines for each of your staff? They'll get monthly or bimonthly reminders that you're supportive of their stretching in their abilities.

13. Make training enjoyable.

Don't just drag some chairs into a circle in the church basement. Decorate around a theme. Provide child care. Send invitations. Be creative! The energy you invest will communicate the importance of training and jazz up the experience without spending a fortune to take your team to Hawaii for a beachfront training session.

14. Integrate mentoring into your training process.

If a volunteer serves as a teacher, arrange for regular visits from a master teacher who'll observe and provide help reaching the next level. If a volunteer makes hospital visits, ask the hospital chaplain to team up with your volunteer for a visit or two, and then talk with your volunteer about how to be even more effective. Training doesn't have to be a separate event hosted quarterly in a special room at church.

15. Build variety into your training.

When you're communicating content, use as many media formats and methods as you're comfortable using. Keep in mind that when people hear information, they retain little of it. When they roll up their sleeves and immediately use that information, it becomes part of who they are.

Use technology that the church already owns. Find out what it takes to plug into the PowerPoint dock or Internet connection, and use the video projection to show video clips. There are a lot of great clips on Youtube you can use.

16. It's okay to repeat yourself.

If you do a session on emergency evacuation procedures, consider following up your formal training with a fire drill followed by a refresher course followed by another fire drill. Over the course of a few months, the information will sink deep into what your volunteers know—and what they've practiced doing. And a practice evacuation costs nothing.

17. Consider "certifying" some positions.

There's nothing wrong with having "usher certification" that demonstrates that the certified usher has been through a training course, been mentored by a certified usher, and has passed a ten-question exam that includes the questions an usher is most likely to be asked.

The cost of developing a certification program? Almost nothing—just the training, the testing, and a certificate designed on your computer.

18. Build feedback loops into your training.

If training sessions are characteristically you talking and everyone else listening, you may be surprised how little training is actually taking place.

The goal of training is for volunteers to retain and use information, not just to be exposed to it. Remember that talking isn't necessarily teaching, and listening isn't necessarily learning.

19. Let volunteers apply new knowledge immediately.

There's a shelf life on learning. Unless volunteers use it fairly quickly, it tends to slip away because it has not been applied. Be intentional about providing opportunities to apply learning quickly!

Best is to actually put new knowledge to use, but a great deal will be retained even if the best you can offer is simulation or practice sessions. Anything that moves theory down to practical application is a plus!

20. Make emotional connections.

Use stories as well as statistics. If you fire off a long string of numbers, you'll see eyes glaze over—fast. Mix it up, and be sure that even statistics are presented in such a way that there's an emotional response on the part of your training audience. You're looking to make an emotional connection, to build on the material being presented, and to add to other, existing interests of your audience.

21. Keep things interesting.

Volunteers who have given up a Saturday for a training session will forgive almost anything except boredom. You forgot to bring a snack—no problem, everyone will live. You ran 10 minutes overtime—well, you'll do better next time.

But if you're boring, you're dead. Beat boredom by being interactive; use group projects and discussions. Design your session so more than one learning style is tapped.

And personalize the training to keep it relevant. Volunteers are much more interested when you're helping them solve an immediate problem than when you're passing on information they don't see an immediate need to have.

> Beat boredom by being interactive.

Find a need, and design training to meet it!

22. Training isn't always the solution.

If you have a volunteer who seems unable to be successful in a role after training, coaching, and several second chances, it's possible that volunteer will never be successful. The task may be beyond the volunteer's ability. You may have misunderstood the volunteer's abilities, skills, or passions for ministry. Move the volunteer to a new role, and start over. Sometimes it's wise to cut your losses.

23. Bring snacks.

Always. There's nothing like a plate of homemade chocolate chip cookies to win a training group over.

24. Use experts.

A sad fact: Everyone knows you, so you must not know much. But if you find someone in a neighboring church who has the same knowledge you have, that person is an expert!

Dig for resource people willing to provide training at no (or low) cost. They're out there. A professional teacher in your church or a neighboring church can speak to classroom discipline. A counselor can share training about conflict resolution or listening. Who has expertise in your circle of acquaintances? You can often find a true expert at a local college or involved in a local church and get the benefit of that person's expertise for the cost of mileage reimbursement and a thank-you gift.

A caution: Knowing something doesn't mean you know how to teach it. You'll need to work with presenters to make sure they design training that's on target.

And a bonus tip:

Keep track. What gets measured gets reported, and what gets reported is usually what matters. Know who comes to training events and who doesn't—and keep track of attendance. If attendance is part of the volunteer's position description, immediately follow up with no-shows to find out why they missed and to arrange make-up training.

There's nothing like watching a session on video to convince a no-show that it would have been more fun to be there in person.

The cost of recording the training session? A call to borrow a flip cam, asking a teenager to do the taping, and you're all set.

10 Training Approaches for Small Churches— and Busy People

How do you keep training sessions from overwhelming your schedule? Here are three ways to keep training in check—but still effective.

Some trainers estimate that preparing a 1-hour training session can take up to 10 hours. When you consider how much research is required to do a needs analysis and then work through designing a session, that estimate doesn't seem far-fetched. In fact, it may be conservative.

So here you are, the lone person responsible for your church's volunteer ministry. Where are you going to find time to create and lead training for the dozen different volunteer positions you have to fill?

And another question: Why should you create a formal youth leader training program when you only need to recruit, place, and train one youth volunteer? It doesn't make sense!

Except it does make sense.

What doesn't make sense is letting a volunteer enter a position for which he or she isn't prepared and then letting the volunteer fail for lack of knowledge or skills, especially when we know we could come alongside the volunteer and help that person flourish in the ministry role.

> " There is never a reason for setting a volunteer up for failure. "

Stand firm on this point: There is never a reason for setting a volunteer up for failure. Never. If a ministry isn't ready to receive a volunteer or a volunteer isn't ready to take on the role, don't force it. The result will be disappointment and failure all the way around.

Which means what? That you have to provide all the training? Not necessarily.

Determining the Need for Specialized Training

You've got volunteers doing everything from accounting to lawn care. How much specific task-related training is worth providing?

Asking these questions will help you make that determination…

- Are there volunteers serving in roles that require continuing education units, licensing, or certification by the government? If so, what responsibility does the church feel for helping volunteers maintain their certification? any? all? You probably can't provide the actual training; the decision you need to make is whether you'll pay for any or all of it since the church benefits from it.

- What are logical groupings of volunteers who need training? For instance, do you have fifteen educators who could use training but just two puppeteers? If you have time to design just a few specialized training sessions, where will you get the "biggest bang for your buck"?

- What new skills and knowledge do volunteers need to master for your ministry to reach a goal that's already in place? For instance, if the church plans to open a day care center and to utilize volunteers in some roles, there are training considerations to address before the day care's doors open for business.

- What funding is available for training?

- Is there expertise your team has developed that can be organized into training that could be provided for other churches? And if so, would charging for that training generate money to support or expand your ministry? What incentives are in place to encourage volunteers to seek additional training? What obstacles are in place that interfere with training? You won't be a happy camper if you prepare training sessions and nobody comes.

Here's where you probably landed after answering those questions: You want trained volunteers, and the benefits that come with training.

Some jobs seem to require very little training.

You don't have time to train everyone.

You aren't sure what to do.

Donna's Experience

Welcome to the club. That's precisely where Donna found herself when she assumed the role of director of volunteer equipping for her church of 200.

"We had most of the programs operating that a church of a thousand has," she says, "which meant we were really stretched on covering the roles."

Donna did what she could, but some positions went unfilled because there wasn't anyone in the church who was appropriately gifted to fill them. In other cases, there were people serving, but only one or two per category.

"I found myself wondering how I could possibly justify writing a training session for Matt, who was responsible for stacking chairs in our worship center after Sunday morning worship celebrations. He put the chairs on a rack and rolled the rack into a closet. What was I supposed to train him to do?"

> How could I possibly justify writing a training session for Matt?

Here's the thing: With the church sitting at an attendance of 200, Matt didn't really need a formal 1-hour training session. Doing a 5-minute demonstration handled it. But if the church grew to a thousand and the 10 rows of chairs multiplied into a sea of chairs, what then?

- Matt would need help. How should he go about recruiting volunteers? scheduling them? supervising them?

- Matt would probably need to lock up the building because he and his crew would take longer to accomplish the task. What responsibilities came with having a key to the worship center?

- Matt would need to do periodic evaluations of his volunteers. How could he do that without them having a position description? And him having one as well?

Because the church was still small, Donna had the luxury of not creating a formal training session. She still needed to create a ministry description, provide an orientation, and train Matt to do the task, and for the moment that was enough.

But if the church grew and Matt's role changed, formal training would be needed. And the lack of it would eventually become obvious. Failing to provide in-depth training is like burying a land mine; sooner or later, it will be triggered.

Because of demands on her time, Donna has found three innovative ways to provide training—including a technique she used to train Matt.

Decide if these techniques will work for you, too…

1. Training Sheila

"A decision to expand our Sunday morning program to include a children's church service threw us for a loop," says Donna. "None of our children's ministry team had ever actually led worship for elementary students."

So Donna called the children's worship team leader at a nearby, larger church. And after Sheila was identified as the person who would be leading the new ministry, Sheila attended a month of services at the other church. "They were incredibly helpful," says Donna. "Sheila got training from their staff and learned what worked and didn't work for them. It shortened our learning curve dramatically. Our program got up and running far quicker because of what Sheila learned."

> Donna called the children's worship leader at a larger church.

Which raises the question: Is your church the best place to get the training your people need? Be open to calling other churches—and being called by other churches in turn. What churches in your community might be willing to help you?

Donna still needed to create position descriptions, but she was able to get some from the other church to adapt.

Donna will also need to eventually create (or have Sheila create) training sessions for additional children's church staff who come into the program, but that can wait until everyone catches their breath.

2. Training Bruce

Donna's church building sat on a corner one block away from a university campus, which meant that you might expect the congregation to have a vibrant outreach to college students.

You'd be wrong.

"Some of our members were students, but given that dorms housing more than two thousand students sat within three blocks, we weren't being very effective reaching them."

The pastor decided to launch a visitation program in the dorms. "We looked around the congregation and found we had a retired military recruiter who was worshiping with us. He knew all the people who ran the dorms, he was used to knocking on doors, and he was passionate about his faith. Perfect, right?"

Perfect, except he didn't want the job.

"He told us he'd retired from knocking on doors. He had zero interest in doing it again, even for the church."

So Donna shifted her request. Instead of actually going on visits, would the man be willing to pass on what he knew to someone else? Would he become a trainer?

> "Perfect, except he didn't want the job."

After some deliberation, the ex-recruiter agreed, and Donna found Bruce, who was willing to go to the dorms and to build a team to go with him but who lacked experience connecting with college students and establishing relationships.

The result was a successful program. And once it was up and running, the ex-recruiter decided to take an active role after all.

Donna arranged for Bruce to receive the training he needed, but not from her. And if you're willing to isolate training into modules, you may find you don't need to do all the training, either.

Bruce needed two sorts of training: how to share his faith, and how to be comfortable inviting students to participate in a program. Donna knew how to deliver the first sort of training, but not the second. That's where the ex-recruiter came in.

In your congregation, are there teachers and principals available who aren't interested in teaching a class—but they'd train teachers? Are there professional salespeople who would be willing to train your ushers how to make eye contact, shake hands, and engage people? Are there counselors who can teach your small group leaders how to actively listen? The possibilities are almost endless.

3. Training Matt

Back to the man with a chair rack and a mission…

Donna recognized the need for Matt to have some help, so she encouraged him to recruit a few chair stackers who could give him a hand, learn the ropes, and then cover for him when he happened to be out of town.

Donna developed a position description, which one of the stackers—the vice-president of a multi-million dollar insurance company whose corporate office was in town—was delighted to receive. He had it framed and hung it in his office as a reminder that service, not status, was the highest calling.

And the formal training session? Donna never developed it.

"I couldn't find a skill gap," Donna reports. "This is a narrow enough task that we can cover it with OTJ—on the job—training. Matt can explain the entire procedure to his helpers in about 5 minutes, so I'm letting orientation take care of the training."

At last look the system is doing fine—chairs get stacked and put away, and nobody has needed a training session to do it.

> "Where can you use OTJ training in your volunteer ministry?"

Where can you use OTJ training in your volunteer ministry? At what point do you need to move past it and structure formal training?

11 Track Your Training

Training isn't cheap, so get the biggest bang for your buck by tracking your volunteers' training history— and planning ahead.

You're ready to do it—make sure every volunteer is trained. You're willing to invest time, energy, and even—perhaps—budget on creating effective training sessions. You've got a dozen or two dozen or two *dozen* dozen volunteers moving through your training sessions.

It's beginning to feel like you're running a university, not a volunteer program.

But can you remember which volunteer has taken which seminar, session, or class? Do you know if you have enough CPR-trained volunteers whose certification is current? Are there enough volunteers who've taken the driver safety course that your insurance agency insists on for adults who transport special-needs kids? Do you know which training sessions are most useful for someone who's volunteering in Christian education as opposed to, say, the Christmas pageant?

Different programs in your church have different training needs. Volunteers themselves have different training needs, depending on the demands of their volunteer roles or their own skill levels. Or new training may be required because somewhere along the way the requirements for being a volunteer receptionist changed, and only those with computer skills need apply.

You need to track the training you provide—on several levels.

- **You need to know which volunteers have completed specific sessions.**

    If completion of specific sessions is a prerequisite for serving in certain roles (for example, "Nursery volunteers must complete the nursery orientation and the infant CPR class"), then you'd better be able to know who's done what, and when. And don't count on being able to remember.

Try this: Recite which courses you took during your last semester of high school. Now list the eight people who sat closest to you in homeroom.

Right—we didn't think you could do it. Few people can. And if you'll put a system in place to track your volunteers' ongoing participation in training, you won't need to remember. You can use those brain cells for more important things, like figuring out where you stashed your yearbook so you can look up the answers to those questions we asked you.

- **You need to know which training sessions have proven to be most helpful to your volunteers.**

  If your most long-term nursery volunteers all credit Janice's training about how babies learn as their motivation for sticking with the program, that's something you want to know. And it's probably a reason you'll want every nursery volunteer exposed to Janice's training program.

  Training has an impact, and it's not only measurable by determining whether the objective was obtained; it's also measurable longitudinally, by seeing how it impacts long-term behavior and attitudes. If you have a tracking system in place, you can see trends develop that will allow you to proactively place people in training sessions.

> "Training has an impact."

Create Tracking Systems

At minimum, create a folder for each volunteer to update which training sessions have been completed, and when. What you place in folders depends in part on where you'll keep them.

If you're planning to include the notes taken during volunteers' placement interviews and the results of background checks, you must treat folders as confidential, keep them in a locked cabinet, and monitor who has access to the keys. Your volunteers were assured of appropriate confidentiality when they were interviewed; you must maintain it.

If you're simply tracking sessions taken and ongoing notes about sessions that might be appropriate, you're probably safe having the information easily accessible. But check with legal counsel first; if all records you maintain are considered personnel files, take appropriate precautions.

And the same holds true if you use computer spreadsheets to track sessions.

- **Track training your volunteers have completed**

  A sample Continuing Education Sheet is available for your adaptation and use on page 201. Create a sheet for each of your volunteers.

  The title of the sheet is strategic; most educators are familiar with the term "continuing education," and it sets an expectation that volunteers will continue to grow in their knowledge and skills.

  Plus, the term is broader than just the training sessions you offer at your church. As you'll see in the next section, continuing education can come from many sources—and it's good for you to note any that volunteers bring to your attention.

  If you have a medical doctor who attends a neurology conference and spends two days learning about how children learn, do you think a distilled version of that information will be of value to your Sunday school teachers? Absolutely! Indicate the doctor's training event on his or her sheet; you may want to tap that expertise later to create a training session.

  Of course, none of your volunteers are accustomed to reporting what happens at work when they go to church. Few of your staff will think to tell you that they were out of town for a convention that included significant training.

  That's why you'll have to ask.

  During the meeting when you introduce the Continuing Education Sheet, suggest examples of how work training might apply to your church's programs and volunteers.

Some possibilities might be…

A police officer who receives training on child safety, who can then provide insight into how your children's ministry department might be better equipped to protect children in its care;

An accountant whose continuing education class includes up-to-date information about what volunteers can and can't deduct as charitable donations when it comes to serving at the church;

A buyer for a craft store who is given a close-up look at new craft materials coming out in the next year and can then suggest decorating items to the vacation Bible school director.

Ask your volunteers what they know and what they're learning that might be helpful to other volunteers. Add a quick comment at staff meetings that you'd like to hear about any training your volunteers have received—any training at all. You may choose to not follow up on some items (the hunter who passed his expert marksman course probably won't be able to turn it into a training session), but you'll know the expertise is available.

You can serve as the center of that information web, but only if you recall what you've been told…which brings you back to filling out your volunteers' continuing education sheets and updating them regularly.

- **Track which training sessions are most useful.**

  This is a three-step process…

  Document what you've done. You first need to document what training has been offered through your volunteer ministry and the content of each session. Without a record of that information, you'll never be able to determine which of those sessions was most valuable.

  If you aren't already capturing notes from each training session, start at once. If possible, videotape or audiotape each session, too. This allows you to have a library of "instant" training sessions for volunteers who enter a ministry and need to get up to speed. It also allows you to know, in two years, what happened in that training session everyone says changed their lives.

Remember how you couldn't recall which training session every volunteer took? You won't remember the content of each training session, either—even the ones you led. Capture the content, and keep it on file.

Create a catalog. Create a catalog of training sessions you offer, and keep it current. Include descriptions of the sessions and what each session's objectives are—why a volunteer would want to attend. Also indicate who leads the session.

If you feel there's a need to offer the session regularly (once per year, once per semester, or whatever), go ahead and schedule it on the church calendar now. Though orientation sessions are often "on demand" sessions, given when the volunteer first signs on, many training sessions can be taken after a volunteer is in place.

You'll need the catalog when you implement the third step in the evaluation process—asking current volunteers to indicate which training sessions were especially helpful to them.

Ask for feedback. Give each volunteer a sheet listing the training sessions he or she has attended, a copy of the catalog, and a copy of the Best Ever Sheet. A sample copy of a Best Ever Sheet is on page 202, and you're welcome to use and adapt it.

The catalog will serve as a memory-jogger for volunteers. It's unlikely volunteers will remember the names of sessions they attended eight months earlier, but they'll probably recall the names of the trainers and the course objectives that were achieved.

Ask volunteers to complete the Best Ever Sheet and turn it in to you. As you collect a number of Best Ever Sheets, look for trends by ministry area and by success of the volunteers.

If your top-performing small group leaders all cite a few training sessions as beneficial, be sure that every small group leader goes through those sessions.

> Look for trends by ministry area and by success of the volunteers.

To be sure, there are variables when it comes to training sessions.

The person presenting can play a huge role in making a session enjoyable and communicating the content effectively.

The relevance of the material may change depending on what's happening in the church or culture.

And the timing of the session can play a role, too. A session on how to lead small groups of children will be far more timely the week before vacation Bible school than during Christmas break. Volunteers who attend will be able to use the learning almost immediately in the summer, and in the winter they'll be distracted by the holiday. But trends will emerge—and only by tracking them can the big picture of what you should put in place as standard training emerge.

Your goal is in several years to determine a baseline of training sessions every volunteer should go through, and a second tier of training for each ministry group.

And may we encourage you to eventually add training sessions that are more for your volunteers than their roles? For instance, most volunteers are busy people. They might appreciate a training session on how to maintain life balance, or a session on time management—anything that helps reduce stress.

Adding a few "personal fulfillment" sessions as elective training will make your volunteer ministry a friendlier place to serve.

Sources for Training and Trainers

One way to add variety to training sessions is to make sure it's not always you leading them. Several sources of alternate training sources have been mentioned already, but for your convenience here's an expanded list. How many of these sources have you tapped?

Community experts—Contact the United Way, fraternal groups, or college instructors who teach courses in areas that are of interest. Not all will have a ready list of experts who are eager to come lead training, but some will. And for the cost of mileage and a warm handshake you can have real experts provide input.

Do a thorough briefing for outside speakers about your group and what to expect. Be clear about your values and the outcomes you want the training to provide. Work with the experts to reach a clear understanding of what they'll cover. And seek permission to record their presentation before the training event itself. Some experts may be uncomfortable in front of a camera.

Inside experts—You have some experts at your church, you know. Be on the lookout for training that your volunteers experience in their professional lives that could easily translate to their volunteer roles—or someone else's volunteer roles. Your doctor who learned about brain research and learning might sing in the choir, but the expertise is relevant to your Christian education department. If the doctor is willing, ask him or her to work with you to create and lead a training session with your children's workers.

> "You have some experts at your church."

Seminars—Take advantage of training offered in your area by Group, other publishers, or Christian organizations.

Training with other churches—If your training session is skill-based rather than centered on knowledge specific to your church, invite other churches to attend. "How to relate to youth" is going to be valuable to youth workers of all denominations, and it will cost you very little more to present the training to a room of 30 people instead of a room of 10.

A bonus: Ask for the same courtesy in return, and take advantage of training provided by other churches.

Books and articles—It's very possible you'll never see the items again, so don't circulate anything you feel you can't live without. But publications that address relevant issues can be shared among those volunteers who could benefit from them. The secret is to attach an interactive routing slip and to make it easy for volunteers to pass along the publications. An interactive routing slip is on page 204 for you to adapt for your use.

If volunteers have a box or a mail slot in the church office, this is fairly simple. If not, as a team work together to create a system for exchanging items in a timely fashion. Or e-mail articles or links to articles so you don't have to worry about items being circulated or returned.

If you discover that many of the helpful articles are from one or two magazines, contact the publisher and ask for a group discount subscription. Then you can distribute the entire magazine to appropriate volunteers.

When these articles or books return to you (think positively!), add them to a permanent library of source material. If they were worth circulating, they're worth keeping.

On the other hand, if you wouldn't keep the information, don't interrupt your volunteers' lives with a request they read it.

Show and Tell—If you or a colleague in the volunteer ministry attends a conference or seminar that's paid for by the church, set it as policy that the person who attends must present what was learned when the person returns. This policy keeps your attendee sharp and on the lookout for usable ideas while at the convention, not lying on the beach instead of attending sessions.

> **Ask for a show and tell session.**

An easy way to position this is to ask for a show-and-tell session that describes three ideas volunteers can put to use immediately and three that should be considered long-term.

Give conference-goers a large tote to fill with materials from the conference vendors, too. Often there are great give-aways that can be used at the church. If the bag gets too cumbersome, it can be shipped to the church instead of being dragged on the plane.

And finally, give your conference attendees 20 or 30 dollars to buy CDs of sessions that were especially useful. Listening to a CD as you drive isn't the same as being there, but it's an affordable way to experience the workshop. And the CDs can become part of your permanent library.

Orientation and Training As a Retention Tool

Does it seem odd to think of your orientation and training as tools that keep volunteers active in your church? It actually makes perfect sense.

The effort you invest in creating outstanding orientation and training opportunities communicates to volunteers. It sends a signal.

It signals that someone—you—notices them and is concerned about their comfort and effectiveness. They know you're willing to go the second mile to see they have the skills and information they need.

It signals that you value them, and that they're part of a team.

It signals that they serve in a church and a ministry program where they're encouraged to grow in their own faith, their own skills, and their own relationship with Jesus.

And who wouldn't want to hang around a place like that?

Your efforts are sending a signal, all right. It's a signal of loving concern. Thanks for what you're doing for and with your volunteers. Together you're accomplishing amazing things.

Onward and upward!

Sample Forms, Letters, and Evaluations

Here's everything you need to launch your recruitment, interviewing, orientation, and training systems.

Copy and adapt any of the forms you find here. They're yours for the taking, so long as you use them in your local church setting. Keep in mind that no form is truly a "one-size-fits-all" solution, so give serious thought to personalizing these forms for your unique situation. Ask someone in your church who has a writing background to work with you to tweak what you find here until it perfectly reflects your church's values and culture.

- Defining the Purpose of Your Volunteer Equipping Ministry
- Determining Your Target Audiences
- Marketing Goals
- Volunteer Benefit Analysis Sheet
- Marketing Message Delivery Plan
- Volunteer Ministries Placement Interviewer—Sample Position Description
- Interview Confirmation Letter—Sample
- Discovering My Abilities, Skills, and Passions
- Interview Form—Sample
- Interview Follow-Up Letter—Sample
- Program Evaluation Form
- Volunteer Handbook Acknowledgement Form—Sample
- Training Session Evaluation
- Volunteer Continuing Education Log Sheet
- Best Ever Evaluation Sheet
- Interactive Routing Slip—Sample
- Volunteer Orientation Guidelines—Sample
- Volunteer Bill of Rights

Defining the Purpose of Your Volunteer Equipping Ministry

Your mission statement:_____

_____

_____

_____

Who does your volunteer ministry serve? _____

_____

_____

_____

What services or products does your ministry provide to those you serve?

_____

_____

What is unique about your ministry?

_____

_____

Your purpose statement: _____

_____

Checklist:

☐ **Your statement of purpose clearly identifies why your volunteer ministry exists.**

☐ **The statement of purpose is inspiring to paid staff, volunteers, and clients.**

☐ **The statement of purpose provides clarity for decision-making.**

Determining Your Target Audiences

Internal audiences: _____

_____

_____

What you *know* about these audiences: _____

_____

_____

What you *assume* about these audiences:

_____

_____

External audiences:_____

_____

What you *know* about these audiences: _____

_____

What you *assume* about these audiences: _____

_____

Checklist:

☐ **You've identified each audience your volunteer ministry needs to address.**

☐ **You've checked what you know against unbiased data (demographic information, church profiles, discussions with church leaders).**

☐ **You've checked what you assume with at least two members of each audience you've identified.**

Marketing Goals

Marketing campaign: _____

_____

_____

As a result of our marketing efforts, what do we want people to *know*?

_____

_____

How will we know we've accomplished this goal? _____

_____

_____

Who is primarily responsible for making this goal happen? _____

_____

_____

As a result of our marketing efforts, what do we want people to *believe*?

_____

_____

How will we know we've accomplished this goal? _____

_____

_____

Who is primarily responsible for making this goal happen?

_____

_____

As a result of our marketing efforts, what do we want people to *do*?

_____

_____

How will we know we've accomplished this goal? _____

_____

_____

Who is primarily responsible for making this goal happen? _____

_____

_____

Checklist:

☐ **Be sure each goal is specific.**

☐ **Be sure each goal is challenging, but attainable.**

☐ **Be sure each goal is measurable.**

☐ **Be sure each goal is connected to a calendar date.**

☐ **Be sure each goal is connected to a person's name.**

Volunteer Benefit Analysis Sheet

Marketing campaign:_____

_____

_____

Volunteer role being filled: _____

_____

_____

What benefits are likely to flow to volunteers who fill this position?

Skill set benefits: _____

Social benefits: _____

Knowledge benefits: _____

Emotional benefits: _____

Spiritual benefits:_____

Recognition benefits: _____

Checklist:

☐ **Each benefit area has at least one benefit flowing from the position description for the role.**

Note that if a benefit area is not represented, it may be perceived as a weakness by potential volunteers.

Marketing Message Delivery Plan

Synopsis of marketing content *(state in two or three sentences)*:

_____

_____

_____

Goal of campaign: _____

Target audience: _____

Proposed channels of communication *(How you intend to deliver your campaign message to your target audience)*: _____

_____

Resources available:

- Finances *(Your budget)*: _____
- Time *(When you need to start and finish)*: _____
- Influencers *(Champions who'll give testimonials or support)*: _____

_____

- Free forums *(Worship services, newsletters, social media...anything you can use without impacting your budget)*: _____

_____

Checklist:

☐ **Be sure your plan is attainable using available resources.**

☐ **Be sure your plan focuses on the campaign goal and each part of your plan makes sense in light of the goal.**

☐ **Be sure you've identified a person who is responsible for each element of your plan.**

Volunteer Ministries Placement Interviewer — Sample Position Description

Job Title: One-to-one Interviewer

Responsible to: Director of Equipping Ministries

Desired Commitment:
- 6 months
- 4-6 interviews (approximately 30 minutes each); attend training session (2 hours) and follow-up meetings (2 hours)

Duties:
- Attend interview training workshop.
- Make appointments with those members you will interview.
- Conduct one-to-one interviews as assigned by Core Team.
- Fill out interview follow-up form after each interview.
- Feed appropriate information back to church staff or volunteer director.
- Attend follow-up meeting to provide feedback to Core Team regarding the interview process.

Desired Qualifications:
- Ability to handle confidential information.
- Experience as a volunteer
- Genuine, caring, "people person" attitude and having an excited commitment to the concept of volunteer ministry
- Good listener
- Familiarity with church programs or willing to learn about those programs
- Interviewing experience helpful but not necessary

Training:
- Interview training workshop provided and required

Interview Confirmation Letter—Sample

Reach Out—Renew—Rejoice!

> *"Each one should use whatever gift he has received to serve others, faithfully administering God's grace in its various forms." (1 Peter 4:10)*

Dear Jack:

Thank you for our conversation about the serving opportunites available through First Church.

We place a high priority on involving members in appropriate, fulfilling ministry. We believe the Bible teaches that all of us are unique and important and that we've each got something valuable to offer in service to others.

It would help me get to know you better if we could talk about some of the following things when we meet on Saturday, July 26, at 2:00 p.m. in the church office:

- What have you done that's given you the greatest satisfaction here at First Church? at another church? in the community?
- What have you always wished you could do?
- What do you enjoy doing in your leisure time?
- Is there a skill you wish you could learn or try?
- What are your hobbies?
- What do you feel you're good at? that you might be good at? that you're not good at?
- What have you done as a volunteer that you enjoyed the least?

And here's a question I'd love to explore with you: What would you like to see happen here at First Church that would have significance for you and/or your family?

That's a lot to think about, but we value your ideas, dreams, opinions, and suggestions. We welcome any questions or concerns you might have about the volunteer opportunities here at First Church.

I look forward to meeting with you, Jack. It's a visit with a wonderful purpose: As members in the body of Christ, we'll be able to better know each other, support each other, and encourage each other in service to others and God.

Sincerely,

Nancy Johnson
Director, Volunteer Ministries
First Church

Discovering My Abilities, Skills, and Passions

Answer the following questions, while thinking of any area of your life that's currently exciting for you—church, career, home, family, school, your social life, leisure time, hobbies, or any other part of your life that energizes you.

1. Some things I believe I do well are: _____

   _____

2. Some things I think I'm not very good at are: _____

   _____

3. If given the chance, I think I might be good at: _____

   _____

4. One new thing I've tried recently that went well was: _____

   _____

5. Who encouraged me to do what I listed in #4? What made the person or persons think I could do it? Does this person or these people encourage me to try new things often?

   _____

   _____

   _____

6. Who are my mentors (my loyal, wise advisers) in life?

   _____

   _____

   _____

Interview Form—Sample

First Church Interview Questionnaire

Name: _____ Spouse: _____

Home phone:_____ Work phone:_____

Cell Phone:_____ E-mail: _____

Address: _____

Birth date:_____ Gender: _____ Marital status: _____

Church member since: _____ Is spouse a member? _____

Children at home (*please list*)

_____ Birth date_____ Church member? _____

_____ Birth date_____ Church member? _____

_____ Birth date_____ Church member? _____

_____ Birth date_____ Church member? _____

Other children not at home, or family ties to <u>First Church</u>.

_____

Have you served in any of the following capacities? (*please check*)

Where and when?

☐ Church board or other
  congregational leadership   _____

☐ Christian education   _____

☐ Youth ministry   _____

☐ Committee work   _____

☐ Usher ministry   _____

☐ Other: _____

Leadership training received at church or work (*please explain*):

_____

_____

Other training received (*such as child abuse training, Stephen Ministries, and other training*):

_____

_____

Are there times of the day or week you are not available?

_____

Worship service you prefer to attend:

_____

Notes:

_____

_____

_____

Permission for information to be entered into the church database (*please sign*):

_____   _____
Signature   Printed name

Today's date: _____   Interviewer: _____

Interview Follow-Up Letter—Sample

Dear Jack,

Thanks so much for meeting with me and agreeing to consider a ministry opportunity at <u>First Church's Preschool Christian Education Department</u>.

That role is supervised by <u>Karen Hedges</u>.

<u>Ms. Hedges</u> will be contacting you by phone in the next week to arrange to meet with you to further explore your volunteering in that ministry. Though it appears that your God-given abilities, interests, and passions for service would be well-used in that ministry, it's a good idea to be sure. Additional discussion will help confirm our thinking.

Again, thank you, <u>Jack</u>. It's exciting to see you step out and serve. God will bless your efforts and help you grow as you serve others!

Though you'll be talking with <u>Ms. Hedges</u>, please call on me if at any time I can be of service to you.

Sincerely,

<u>Nancy Johnson</u>
<u>Director, Volunteer Ministries</u>
<u>First Church</u>

Volunteer Handbook Acknowledgment Form—Sample

Please complete this form and return it to the Director of Volunteer Ministries. Before you can be placed in a volunteer role, this form must be on file in the Volunteer Ministries office.

Please read this handbook carefully. It contains the policies, procedures, philosophy, and expectations relating to volunteering at First Christian Church. When you've completed reviewing this handbook, please complete and sign the following statement. Return it to _____, the Director of Volunteer Ministries.

A copy of this acknowledgement form appears at the back of this handbook for your records.

I, _____, acknowledge that I've received and read a copy of First Christian Church's Volunteer Handbook. The Handbook contains the policies, procedures, philosophy, and expectations relating to volunteering at First Christian Church.

I've familiarized myself, at least generally, with the contents of this handbook. My signature below acknowledges that I understand the information contained in this handbook and agree to comply with it.

I understand this handbook isn't intended to cover each and every situation I may encounter as a volunteer, but is intended to be guide.

Signature _____

Date: _____

Program Evaluation Form

We're always looking for ways to improve our orientation program. Your filling out this evaluation helps us find ways to make the experience even better in the future.

Did the orientation program meet your expectations? Why or why not?

_____

_____

Was the orientation program complete?

_____

_____

What information did you find most helpful?

_____

_____

What information did you feel was missing?

_____

_____

What questions do you have that weren't answered?

_____

_____

What would you add to improve the orientation program?

_____

What would you remove to improve the orientation program?

_____

Training Session Evaluation

Please answer the following questions about today's session to help today's trainer improve future training sessions.

Date:_____ Session topic: _____

Name of trainer: _____ Your name: _____

How long have you been a volunteer at [name of your church]?

_____

1. What was the main objective of this session?

_____

_____

2. What were other objectives you remember?

_____

_____

3. How would you rate the pace of today's session?

Too slow   Slow   About right   Fast   Too fast

Why was that?

_____

_____

4. How challenging did you find today's session?

Not at all   Not very   Neutral   Somewhat   Very

Why was that?

_____

_____

5. How relevant was the training to needs you're feeling now?

Not at all   Not very   Neutral   Somewhat   Very

How could the training have been more relevant to your needs?

_____

_____

6. In your estimation, how well prepared was the trainer?

Not at all   Not very   Neutral   Somewhat   Very

Why was that?

_____

_____

7. Please write your thoughts or questions about any part of the session about which you're still unclear:

_____

_____

8. Please offer any suggestions or further comments regarding this session:

_____

_____

9. What other issues or items would you like to address on another day?

_____

_____

Volunteer Continuing Education Log Sheet

Name of volunteer: _____

Volunteer positions held: Dates:

_____   _____

_____   _____

_____   _____

_____   _____

Church training sessions attended: Date:

_____   _____

_____   _____

_____   _____

_____   _____

External training attended (describe):   Date:

_____   _____

_____   _____

_____   _____

_____   _____

Best Ever Evaluation Sheet

You're the best—and we want to know how you got that way!

In an effort to provide the best training sessions possible, we like to find out what training is most helpful and has had the greatest impact on your effectiveness.

Please take a few minutes and consider the list of training sessions you've attended. If you can't remember what was covered at each session, consult the Training Session Catalog. Then answer the following questions as honestly as you can.

Return this sheet to _____ as soon as possible.

Thank you.

1. Which training session was most memorable for you?

_____

Why?

_____

_____

_____

2. Which training session was most relevant to you?

_____

Why?

_____

_____

_____

3. Which training session provided information or skills you've used most often?

_____

What is that information or those skills?

_____

_____

_____

4. Which training session would you recommend to someone else entering our area of ministry?

_____

Why?

_____

_____

_____

5. Which training session seemed least helpful to you?

_____

Why?

_____

_____

_____

Interactive Routing Slip—Sample

(Notice how there's accountability built into this routing slip—and a chance to write a review.)

Volunteer Ministry Routing Slip

The attached published piece is making the rounds…but not if you slow it down! Please read the attached and add your comments within one week. Then slip it into the Volunteer Office mail slot of the next person on the list.

Thank you!

Mary Jones
Volunteer Director
Date: _____

To:	Date received:	Date passed along:
Jackie Sampson	_____	_____
Aaron Loop	_____	_____
Jeff Knowles	_____	_____
Jim Wood	_____	_____
Jodi Forbes	_____	_____
Shanell Frahm	_____	_____
Brian Shiazi	_____	_____
Janelle Spencer	_____	_____

Share your comments below. Write your initials after your comments, please.

A WOW! idea I found:

_____

_____

Volunteer Orientation Guidelines—Sample

First Christian Church Volunteer Orientation
Nursery Guidelines

What a blessing you'll be to parents as you provide a caring, nurturing, Christ-centered experience for their infants as parents worship. And you'll help babies associate feeling safe and secure with being at church.

Our first concern is safety. The following policies will help us make our nursery safe for babies and nursery workers alike.

- Nursery staff responsible for working an assigned shift must provide staffing or find a replacement from the list of approved substitutes. If a husband and wife are scheduled to work together and neither can come, then they must find two replacements. Notify the nursery director of any staffing changes.

- Three adults will work in the nursery on Sunday mornings (a nursery supervisor, an infant staffer, and a toddler staffer). On Wednesday nights, two adults will work in the nursery (a nursery supervisor and one infant staffer). This ratio must be maintained—no exceptions.

- Youth volunteers will be limited to one at any given time.

- Only the posted number of babies and toddlers can be in the nursery at any one time. If more children are presented, do not admit them until a certified nursery staff member has joined the existing staff to maintain the posted ratio of children/staff. Never exceed the posted ratio.

- Nursery staff must arrive 20 minutes before the Sunday service, Wednesday night program, or special service. On Sundays arrive at 9:10 a.m., and on Wednesdays arrive at 6:25 p.m.

- All nursery staff will wear name tags and greet each parent and child warmly.

- On a child's first visit to the nursery, the parent must fill out a Nursery Information Sheet, which will then be kept on file in the nursery cabinet for future reference.

- Give parents a copy of the Nursery Handbook when they check their child in for the first time.

- No male volunteers are allowed to change babies' diapers.

- Parents will sign three adhesive tags when they check in children. Give one tag to the parent, affix one to the child's back, and put the third tag on the child's diaper bag.

- Parents of infants will complete the Infant Information Sheet when they check babies into the nursery.

- Use the digital pager system to notify parents to return to the nursery if necessary. Nursery supervisors have all been trained how to use it, and instructions are posted by the pager console. Nursery supervisors have the authority to decide when parents need to be notified.

- If a child is hurt but not seriously enough to page the parent, a parental notification form will be completed by the nursery supervisor on duty and given to the parent. A copy of the document will be kept in the church office.

- Diaper changing procedures are posted.

- The sickness policy is posted at the nursery door where both staff and parents can easily see it. Enforce the policy—no exceptions. If a child is turned away from the nursery, give the parent a copy of the policy. Fire and tornado procedures are posted, and two drills will be held annually.

- All nursery staff must complete the required background check and the three-hour First Christian Church Certification Program.

- Pictures of the nursery staff and their certification information will be posted to reassure parents of our preparation and professionalism.

- Children will remain inside the nursery until retrieved by an authorized person. Parents must have their retrieval tag, which must match the child's back tag. Parents must sign out their child.

- At the end of each nursery session, the nursery supervisor will complete a nursery supply summary and leave it in the church office. Nursery staff will also put clean bedding on any cribs that have been used. Deal with used bedding as instructed on the posted laundry instruction sheet.

- At the end of each nursery session, toys will be cleaned with a diluted bleach solution of 10:1 water/bleach ratio.

Volunteer Bill of Rights

I have the right to…

- Have my volunteer experience in the church encourage a healthy relationship with Jesus Christ.
- Use my God-given abilities, skills, and passions in significant ministry that gives something to the corporate body of Christ.
- Be respected as a full partner in ministry.
- Be young, be old, be any age, and still valued in ministry.
- Be placed in a ministry role based on my gifts and abilities, not my church's need to find warm bodies to fill a slot in the organizational chart.
- Have a position description that provides me with the information I need to know whether I'm doing what's most important for me to be doing.
- Be provided with the resources and training I need to be successful.
- Receive regular evaluations so I can know how I'm doing and where I can improve.
- Serve in an environment where I'm well aware of the safety risks.
- Be respected if I say no to a request to serve in a specific volunteer role.
- Be valued—as a child of God and part of the body of Christ.
- Set boundaries that allow me a healthy work/life balance.
- Be retained as a volunteer not by guilt, but by the joy of serving others, serving God, and serving the church.

For more **amazing resources**

visit us at
group.com...

...or call us at
1-800-447-1070!